SCANDALOUS

SCANDALOUS

Laura D

Published by Virgin Books 2009

2 4 6 8 10 9 7 5 3 1

Copyright © Laura D 2008

English Translation Copyright © Adriana Hunter 2009

First published in Great Britain in 2009 by
Virgin Books
Random House, 20 Vauxhall Bridge Road
London SW1V 2SA

www.virginbooks.com

www.rbooks.co.uk

Addresses for companies within The Random House Group Limited can be found at:
www.randomhouse.co.uk/offices.htm

The Random House Group Limited Reg. No. 954009

A CIP catalogue record for this book is available from the British Library

Trade paperback ISBN 9780753515556

The Random House Group Limited supports The Forest Stewardship Council [FSC], the
leading international forest certification organisation. All our titles that are printed on
Greenpeace-approved FSC-certified paper carry the FSC logo.
Our paper procurement policy can be found at www.rbooks.co.uk/environment

Typeset by TW Typesetting, Plymouth, Devon
Printed in the UK by CPI Bookmarque, Croydon, CR0 4TD

To my sister in the shadows . . .

'One word written on this page, and the whole thing starts ... The fusion between ink and paper, between you and me ... Love, one person transcending another, the other responding. The moment where the two become 'one'; writing, our story, this book. This moment that sends tremors through me. How real the words and facts are, the horror set down in writing ... the horror of a quotient of students' time ... A book, about Laura, but Laura is more than one person ... She's too many people at the same time, we need to open our eyes and react ...'

This book was written in collaboration with Marion Kirat, aged 23, a translation student.

CONTENTS

Don't Close Your Eyes

I SLOWLY PUT THE LETTER DOWN on the edge of the bed. Without thinking I take off my top and, not waiting for any reaction from him, slide my jeans down over my thighs. I lower myself in what I hope is a slightly languid movement to get them right off.

He can't take his eyes off me, his mouth is gaping. I can see the beginnings of an erection beneath his jogging pants.

My bra, cotton knickers and stockings are now the only things hiding my anatomy. I stand in front of him with my hands behind my back, offering him all this intimacy. I'm the child-woman, Nabokov's Lolita, and he loves it. I'm completely disconnected from reality. This is like torture for me but I dispel it with a giggle. I've got so many complexes about my body, even though it's so slim now, and I'm genuinely finding this situation confusing. He doesn't move and hasn't said anything for quarter of an hour.

He takes a deep breath and begins to open his lips. Go on, say something.

'Wow!' he manages to exclaim quickly.

And that's it. One exclamation. No one could under-stand how I suddenly feel. All at once my body is filled with hope and a sort of happiness. With just one word and in a fraction of a second, this man I've never met before has succeeded where dozens of others have failed: making me realise my body's attractive. Why did it have to be him? I can't answer that, it's just inexplicable. All I know is that it's the first time I've heard and accepted a compliment. That's when I start thinking of him as a man and not some great creep who wants to put his mitts all over me. He must have seen strings and strings of girls but he can still be impressed.

We give each other a knowing smile and something oddly like trust is reached between us.

'This is exactly the sort of reason I don't like "profes-sionals". They can't have that innocent look you've got.'

My name is Laura, I'm nineteen. I'm a modern languages student and I have to prostitute myself to pay my way through uni.

I'm not the only one. Apparently there are 40,000 female students who do what I do. It all followed its own peculiar logic, and I didn't even realise I was falling.

I wasn't born with a silver spoon in my mouth. I've never known luxury and wealth but until this year I've not wanted for anything. My eagerness to learn and my own convictions always persuaded me my student years would be the best and most carefree of my life. I would never have thought my first year at uni would turn into a real-life nightmare and see me running away from my own hometown.

At nineteen, you don't turn to prostitution for pocket money. You don't sell your body just to treat yourself to clothes or buy cups of coffee. You do it if you really have to, convincing yourself it's only temporary, just until you've paid the bills and the rent, and bought some food. Student prostitutes aren't the ones you see in the street. And they're not drug addicts, illegal immigrants or from poor backgrounds. They may have white skin, be French through and through and come from families on modest incomes. All they have in common is the desire to pursue their studies in a country where further education is becoming more and more expensive. The story you are about to read takes place in a large French city. I've called it V to protect my parents. They mustn't know. Ever. I'm their almost perfect little girl. Stubborn but not a slapper.

Of course you could criticise me for not holding down some menial job to keep me out of debt. Most student prostitutes – and this is true of me too – have a little job on the side but still can't stay out of the red. Prostitution and its mind-boggling rates are far too much of a temptation when you're short of money and need some in a hurry.

This is my story: it isn't easy for me to open up about it but my main aim is to expose the hypocrisy surrounding student prostitution. The precarious living conditions for students – of both sexes – in this day and age shouldn't be ignored any longer. At the moment too few people know how terrible they are.

This is my testimony, and it is intended as a wake-up call to bring about changes so that impoverished students never have to sell their bodies to pay for their studies. So that people aren't only shocked by stories of dubious practices in *other* countries but also concentrate their efforts on what is happening in France.

And, finally, so that this is never allowed to happen again, so that people don't just close their eyes to it.

Chapter 1

Enrolling

4 September 2006

I WALK CALMLY ACROSS the campus of V University. Today is no ordinary day because I'm enrolling in modern languages: Spanish and Italian.

Two weeks ago I received a letter telling me I had to be at the university's administrative office at 2.30 p.m. without fail, to submit my application form and get my student card. Filled with excitement, I quickly got together all the documents I needed. There's a lot of paperwork involved, but I managed in the end. The best bit was writing down my grades for my Baccalaureate because it marked the end of an era in a such a concrete way. I also nipped down into the Métro to take some photos – which show me wearing a big smile ... a triumphant smile.

When I got up this morning I studied my route on the Métro to be sure I got to the university on time. I really didn't want to miss the enrolment. I even cheated public transport because I didn't have enough money for my ticket. I promised myself I wouldn't do it again, and would get myself a season ticket, however much it cost. I'm convinced uni's going to make a lot of changes in my life.

I couldn't sit still on the Métro, too excited at the thought of seeing the place where I'd be studying and spending so much of my time. My MP3 player, which I'm usually hooked up to, couldn't soothe my agitated enthusiasm. I even checked three times that I'd got all the papers for my enrolment. I couldn't bear to think of getting there and being told: 'I'm sorry but your records aren't complete. We can't give you your card. You'll have to come back.' No, today was the day I would become a student and that was that.

I was so nervous I very nearly missed my stop. A group of teenagers laughing and talking woke me from my daydreaming at the last minute. They were jostling to get off which reminded me that I needed to get out there too. I'm going to have to get used to my new status: I'm a student now, not a schoolgirl. I'm eighteen and a half.

I arrived on the campus at bang on two o'clock. I didn't really know where to go from the Métro station so I followed the group of students. Now that I'm here I've got some time to spare so I'm having a bit of a walk round to explore the place. I find a map on a board and have a look to find out exactly where I am so I don't get lost. The campus is like a whole village, there are even signposts indicating different buildings. On the map I find the place I will have my lectures: 'Faculty of

Languages, Building F'. Building F, so that's where I'll be for the year. Right now I can't wait to get to know it, to go up and down the steps like an old hand, to know which shortcuts to take to get there. I can't wait to be part of that world.

I decide to have a quick look at the building before enrolling. It wouldn't be right to go home without seeing where I'm going to work on my degree over the next three years. Once outside, I screw up my eyes in the September sun, a memory of the summer that's just gone. It's a pretty boring building, but I don't care. It looks like the beginning of the rest of my life to me.

I have to admit I chose modern languages a bit by default. I wanted to focus on marketing and go to a college that would give me the best possible education. I've always had a lot of get-up-and-go and I like responsibility. I like constant stimulation and the challenge of sales. I also think I wanted the quickest route to having a clear idea of the world of work. I wanted to be really well prepared for my future job. I needed a complete break from the school environment, which was an ordeal for me with its nannying and childishness. And, let's be honest, it can prove much easier finding work after going through business school than university. Work that pays well too.

But that dream's out of reach at the moment. Business school is far too expensive for me. And taking out a loan means making a commitment over several years, which I can't afford. Deep down, I don't think they would even have accepted my application. On top of the overall

7

reimbursement, I can't even make monthly payments regularly right now. So I've given up on that idea and made the strategic move of launching myself into modern languages. I'm still convinced that, with my degree in Spanish and Italian, I could change tack and go to business school where modern languages are vital. Especially as the Latin American economy has expanded so quickly in the last few years and, with my Spanish and Italian, I'd hit the ground running. And, who knows, I might overtake all the others with my cultural baggage as an extra. Standing outside Building F, I've got a head full of dreams.

No one needs to feel sorry for me. I've always had clothes on my back and food on my plate. But I don't know what it's like not to have to think about money. My father works in a factory and my mother's a nurse. They both earn bang on the minimum wage, with two children to bring up. Just enough to make ends meet but never any surplus. I'm not entitled to a grant because I'm one of the countless students who fall between two stools: a long way from what could be called rich, but not poor enough to get student funding. After adding together my parents' two incomes, the State deems that they can support my needs. No way out: I'll have to make do with what we haven't got.

I cut my walk short because I really want to get to the office on time. I can't wait any longer, I want my student card in my hand. I'm almost running.

When I get there I'm confronted with a queue of people which winds its way outside the building. I join it patiently, like the good newcomer I am. But they did say 2.30 p.m. *without fail*. This is my first glimpse of student life, which can so often be boiled down to queuing up at some admin desk for hours.

Just as I'm taking my place in the queue, two girls in different coloured T-shirts literally throw themselves at me.

'Hi, are you a first year?'

'Yes, how about you?' I say with a rather surprised smile.

One of the girls looks at me oddly. That wasn't the reply she was expecting and she apparently has no intention of having a conversation with me. Still, she very soon smiles back: I'm going to be easy prey.

The only reason they approached me was to get me to subscribe to a student payment scheme. I quickly gather from their patter that they're doing this job before the term begins and are paid on commission. They're clearly in competition – if not at war – because, although not actually violent, they keep interrupting each other and almost pushing each other over in their efforts to get my attention. I'm not really sure what I should do, this is all new to me. They're talking so quickly and confusingly I'm only getting every other word. They're both so keen to make the most convincing pitch that they've become completely incomprehensible. I just enjoy the surreal spectacle, although I do feel sorry for them. They're doing this to make a bit of money and I bet they're sweet as pie in everyday life.

'So, have you chosen then?'

The two wrestlers stand looking at me. The bout is over and they now want my judgement to decide the outcome. I haven't listened to a word.

'Umm ... it's just ... I've already got a payment scheme.'

Yes, obviously, that's a good excuse. One of them, clearly disappointed and reckoning she shouldn't waste any more time on me, walks off straight away. The other gives up on me a few minutes later, still trying one last time to persuade me that, sometimes, two policies are better than one, and the one I have isn't the best and *so if you'd like to reconsider your choice for a moment, you'd soon realise* ... blah blah blah.

Faced with an argument so devoid of common sense, I move away to get back in line. It's two thirty, the exact time of my appointment, but I'm sure it wouldn't be right to jump the queue to get to the office, however convincing my explanations. So I decide to wait meekly, taking up my place behind a hugely tall boy. I peer at his appointment card which is just like mine. The words '2 o'clock' are written in red felt-tip right in the middle of the page. Two o'clock! How long has he been here, then?

To one side I can hear the voice of experience from some old hands in their fourth or fifth year, grumbling about how slowly the queue's moving. It must be the same every year. But who cares! I haven't got the urge or the energy to get wound up today. So I don't throw a fit or join in the general complaining.

After half an hour, though, I do wonder whether I've

been forgotten. I spot a man wearing a badge with the official university logo on it, and grab him as he passes.

'I'm sorry to disturb you, but I had an appointment at two thirty. I've been waiting nearly half an hour.' As I speak I wave my letter at him.

'Yes,' he says contemptuously, not even looking at it, 'like everyone else.'

'So? Should I go on waiting? Will I really get in there today?'

'We're doing what we can.'

We're doing what we can ... That's not much of a reply, is it? I've just had my first confrontation with the university's admin department and it's not really a victory, or a relief.

Faced with such an evasive reply, I make up my mind to carry on waiting. I'm annoyed with myself for not bringing a book; I could have spent the time intelligently. I rummage through my bag, but find nothing, not even a newspaper or a stupid leaflet to read. I regret sending those two girls packing so quickly; I could at least have taken one of their brochures, it would have kept me busy for five minutes.

Stupidly, I've dressed up for today. I've put on very old high-heel shoes, as if I were going to an important interview. But standing here in the queue I hate myself for choosing them. If I dared, I'd take them off and go barefoot.

After waiting an hour and a half I finally get to the office. I look at all the windows to see which one is free first. I mutter to myself, fed up with today. I'm not in a good mood any more; I just want to pick up my card and go.

A young woman waves me over at last. I launch myself at her with a smile on my face, glad it will soon be over. She looks at me as if I've just made a pathetic joke and no one's laughing but me. Not really helpful for getting your spirits back up.

We come to the delicate question of my payment.

'Are you paying by cheque?'

Yes, my mother made the cheque out last week. A blank cheque. I can still hear her words: 'Now, be careful, Laura, make sure you don't lose it! Just imagine if someone found it!' I've always had a feel for money and, as soon as that cheque was in my hand, I gauged how powerful it was. I put it carefully into a wallet and put that into a drawer of my desk which locks with a key. I'm the only person who can open it and, even though I do trust my boyfriend who I live with, I'd rather take every precaution. You never know.

'Yes, by cheque.'

'So, as you don't have a grant but you do have a student payment scheme, that makes a total of 404.60 euros.'

What a ridiculous total! I hand her the cheque, trying to hide my smirk. Without a word, she stamps my papers, scribbles signs all over them, and points to the booth for student cards. The whole thing is over in two minutes.

The man in charge of cards is no more friendly than her, and practically snatches my school attendance certificate from my hand. In one mechanically regulated move, he prints my student card onto plastic, hands it to me and snatches the next certificate.

I couldn't care less now, I've got my student card at last. This is it, a new chapter of my life is beginning. I feel confident and serene, holding my future in my own two hands, on this stupid bit of plastic.

Laura D. First year of Modern Languages Spanish.
Classy.

I head back to the Métro, relieved.

Chapter 2

A Stipulation

8 September 2006

AFTER WORKING A FULL DAY at the restaurant I walk back into the apartment where I live with my boyfriend, Manu. We've being going out for a year and moved in together two months ago.

At the time I was desperately trying to solve the problem of where I could live for the start of the academic year. I had no money at all and my parents couldn't help me financially. On top of that, they don't live in V but, ever since I got my Baccalaureate results, I've known I would have to study here. Manu's been living here since he started his physics course and I was really happy to be joining him. So I started looking for an apartment, skimming through the small ads at the student welfare office to find a cheap little room. I soon realised that an actual apartment was far too expensive, not to say completely out of the question. I just wanted a roof over my head, but even that seemed out of reach. I wasn't looking for anything swanky; my budget wouldn't allow for that, anyway.

I'd come to a dead end. Because I wasn't entitled to a grant, I didn't get any help from the State, and that meant no help for accommodation either. The welfare office favoured people with grants for places in student lodgings, and my parents really couldn't put up 200 euros a month for rent. Apart from finding a job or giving up on uni, I couldn't see how to make it work. Plenty of students manage jobs at the same time as studying, but they are often the ones who fail exams or give up during the course of the year. I couldn't abandon my studies, I knew my future was at stake. Giving in now and finding work would mean drawing a line under my ambitions.

I carried on looking frantically for a miracle in the pages of free papers. At the same time I even went to hostels for the homeless to get information about them. I tried to convince myself it would be my only chance of going to uni and that, once I got there, I could try to find something else. But the thought of spending a night in one of those places made me shudder, it just seemed so degrading.

I was beginning to despair of finding an acceptable solution and one day when I was crying with frustration Manu jumped at the opportunity.

'We could live together! It would be great! Between us we could pay a reasonable rent and we'd be together the whole time!'

His eyes were shining. I liked the idea, but my financial problems stood in the way.

'Manu, look, I really can't. I haven't got any money. I've hardly got enough for a room, so a whole apartment . . .'

'You could get a part-time job, uni won't take up all that much time.'

I explained my reservations. Manu's family is comparatively well off and he doesn't always realise all the expenses I have to cover myself. To convince me I could combine my studies with paid work, Manu showed me the university site with timetables on it. I had a lot of lectures but it was workable. I was seduced by this little glimpse of the dream he was offering me.

'You see, you can do it. I'm sure you can. Go on, say yes! It would be so good to be together the whole time. And, basically, you haven't got any choice.'

It was true: I didn't really have a choice. I was so happy I jumped into his arms, and I moved into his apartment the very next day. It was complete luxury for me: not just a bedsit but a one-bedroom apartment in the centre of V. I felt like a princess in that palace! I dumped my two heavy suitcases by the door and started twirling round the apartment, making him dance with me.

My parents were relieved when they heard our solution, even though they're not very keen on Manu. They preferred this to knowing their daughter was doing some moronic job or, worse, sleeping on the streets.

All through the summer I worked in a restaurant just

downstairs from our apartment so that I could at least pay for food. The little money I had left over constituted pocket money.

That's our deal: he pays the rent and the bills, and I take care of the rest, given my financial situation. In fact, although he hasn't told me, I know perfectly well that he's not actually paying the rent. His mother gives him enough to pay for everything, plus a handsome chunk of spending money, every month. I never bring the subject up; I love him too much and, as I'm living in his apartment, I think it's quite right that I should contribute to expenses as much as I can. Anyway, I make do. Sometimes when I go home I load up with whatever's in the fridge or with things my mother gives me. Through the summer it all worked perfectly: we were happy like that, cobbling together little meals for the two of us and occasionally going out for a drink with friends. Most of the time we stayed in watching TV, me nestling in his arms, him always with a joint in his mouth. I was taking my first real bite at life, with my boyfriend by my side, and everything seemed so much easier.

This evening I've come home from work exhausted having done two extra hours which I know I won't be paid for. I'm being completely exploited in this job but so far it's the only solution I've managed to find to guarantee my financial contribution. I also know that, if I do this job all through the year, I'll be tired the whole time but, for now, I don't really have an option. I'll find something else when I've got my actual timetable, and I know exactly when my lectures are.

Manu's here, in front of the TV. I say a happy, bouncy 'hello' as I sit down next to him and give him a big kiss on the mouth. Something strange happens: he doesn't return my enthusiasm.

'What's going on? Is everything OK?'

'Yes, I'm fine,' he says evasively.

'Are you sure? You don't seem . . .'

Manu turns off the TV and looks at me at last. He hesitates for a moment, then suddenly makes up his mind to speak. 'Laura, we're going to live together this year, and I want you to contribute to the rent.'

I pause for a moment, still looking him in the eye. 'Yes, I understand. But I don't make much money at the restaurant. How much do you want from me?'

'Half the rent, 300 euros. You see, I'm not going to be able to do it on my own . . .'

On his own! Liar! He knows perfectly well that I get only just that much from my waitressing and, if I gave it to him, I wouldn't have anything left. Trying to keep my courage up, I tell myself it's high time to give up waitressing and find another job.

'OK,' I say, 'but I think I'll have to find a different job.'

'Yes, I think you're right. And, for the shopping, we'll take it in turns every other week, is that all right?'

Now he's asking me to do the shopping too? I can't believe it.

A lack of money always puts people in such an awkward situation that they don't dare reply. I have to agree, though: 'OK,' I say, 'whatever you say.'

I sit back down on the sofa and turn on the TV so I

don't have to talk. It's the only thing I can think of to end the embarrassed silence between us. At the end of the evening I go to sleep in his arms to persuade myself this whole question of money is fine and needn't come between us.

Two days later I sign up with a telesales company for a part-time job.

Chapter 3

Term Time

17 September 2006

TIMETABLE IN HAND, I have to run so I don't miss my first lecture. I've only just left the secretaries' offices where I've signed up for my course. There I was, thinking all the admin was over and done with after that endless waiting the other day – how wrong I was!

After the administrative enrolment I had to go to the modern languages building and sign up for my course. I have only twenty hours of lectures and tutorials spread out over the week. I've been waiting impatiently for this timetable so that I can organise my life and structure it. I'll be able to carry on working as well as doing my studies. I can call the telesales company first thing tomorrow morning to go over my hours of work.

The whole process was quite speedy and they were quick to give me my timetable but I'm now late for my first commitment. A glance at the piece of paper tells me

I need to get to the third floor for a lecture on Spanish civilisation. I run up the stairs, eager to learn.

I slip into the room quietly – the other students are already sitting at desks – and mumble an inaudible 'Sorry I'm late.' The lecturer flicks his eyes over me and picks his register back up.

'And you are?'

'Laura, Laura D.'

He scribbles something on the page and nods at me to sit down. I choose a chair next to another girl; there are many more girls than boys in the room, and probably in the whole year group.

The lecturer asks us to fill out a form so that he can get to know us. Another wretched form! So far it's not so different from school; they're bound to ask for one in every lesson. By the end of the week I'll be doing them in two seconds flat.

The form includes a space for 'career plans'. I ponder this question for a long time. Do I know what I really want to do? I want to go into business, yes, but in what field exactly? I've got very clear ideas about the sort of responsibilities that would suit me best but is there a recognised name, a particular job description for that? I write down all my dreams, reveal my every expectation for this stranger. Something's missing.

I chew my pencil and gaze up at the ceiling. A few minutes later I add the last few words to my inventory of dreams for the future:

Live life to the full.

Of course, this isn't the sort of reply the lecturer is

expecting, if he actually is expecting anything in particular, but it's the most appropriate one for me.

The lecture begins and, with every passing minute, I thank my lucky stars for the gift of being here in this room. My mother had to shell out more than 400 euros for me to be here but she did it without a moment's hesitation, knowing full well my future depended on it – she's always wanted the best for her daughters. I'm going to learn and I'm going to do well.

The whole lecture is given in Spanish. My father is Spanish and, even though he's never spoken to me in his mother tongue, I've learned it when we've spent holidays with his family.

The lecturer hands out a sheet with a list of books we'll need for the year.

'I need you to be very conscientious. If you want to do well, you'll have to read all of them, and read them carefully, making lots of notes.'

I drink in his words. Yes, of course I'll read them all, I've always loved reading, that's no problem!

'There are some you won't find in the library. I keep asking for them but they never seem to come so you'll have to pay for them yourselves, come to some agreement to share them . . .'

Erm, that bit isn't quite so appealing. Foreign language books are always very expensive, at least fifteen euros each, and if I've got to buy several I'll never be able to cover the cost.

I look at the sheet, worried about how exhaustive it is, and grind my teeth when I see there are about ten books that need buying. I shove it into my bag quickly, not wanting it to ruin the day. There's plenty of time to think about it later.

'On another note, I won't tolerate repeated unjustified absence. After three absences I will not allow you to sit the exam in my subject.'

That's clear, to the point and precise. It's my choice if I really want to succeed or not. The ball's in my court.

The hour is soon over; I wasn't bored for a single second, not like school when I checked my watch every five minutes. I go to the next lecture and this time I see a proper amphitheatre for the first time. I'm so impressed it takes my breath away, and I'm not the only one: lots of us stop for a moment to admire the huge lecture theatre. Only the people taking the year again are quick to find a seat. For them, this is like the enrolment, they know the ropes and can afford to be laid-back.

I look around me – I already know I'm going to love learning in here. I'll be just one needle well hidden inside a haystack, no one will notice me or know me. Lecturers won't stop mid-sentence to comment on my last home-work. University is a service: we are offered lectures and we are free to choose whether we attend them, free to take them as we see fit. University gives you a sense of responsibility: I know I'm just a number in amongst so many others, but right now I have to choose whether I'm going to take it on. I like feeling that I'm seen as an adult already.

I've finally got it, a true break with school. Even after just one day here I can feel everything's going to be different. My last year at school left indelible marks and made me suffer in ways I won't have to here, I'm sure of that.

I can remember one time during that last year when a history teacher publicly humiliated me in front of the whole class by having a go at me personally. He sprang a test on us and when I got a very mediocre mark he told me I was 'useless' – to which I replied by blinking slowly with utter indifference. I could handle his remarks about me perfectly well, that didn't bother me at all because I had absolutely no interest in the man and he always treated me like a little girl. The real problem was what happened next.

'No response, Laura? Well, I'm not going to congratulate you. I think you'll have to have a serious rethink about your future which is looking extremely shaky as things stand at the moment.'

Such cruelty for my first and only below-average mark! But he didn't stop at that.

'Face it, you're totally undisciplined and you don't take your schoolwork seriously. We only reap what we sow, Laura. Your parents must be very irresponsible . . .'

When I heard the word 'parents' my heart missed a beat. What right did this man have to judge my family, going on just one simple mark? I went wild instantly. The girl at the next desk tried to hold me back but it was too late, the fury was already running through my veins and before the inquisitor-teacher had time to respond I hurled the desk and everything on it to the floor. I suffer from anxiety attacks but I've never had one as bad as that day. I grabbed my bag on the hoof and ran from the room.

The next day I signed up for my Baccalaureate as an independent candidate. I couldn't stand the childish atmosphere there a minute longer so I walked out of the place once and for all. I now realise I overreacted and should have swallowed my pride, but at the time I just couldn't. My parents didn't understand at all and, at first, they thought it would be a short-lived drama but, when I stopped getting up early in the mornings and when I got the confirmation for my application as an independent candidate, they realised how serious my decision was. They still carried on waking me every morning, shaking me to get me up for school, but I didn't go. My mother begged me to start lessons again, she even cried.

'You're completely mad! You'll ruin everything! Laura, please, your work's too important to drop it just like this, on a whim. You won't get anywhere without your Bac. You can't just give up like this, not three months before your Bac.'

I've never admitted to my parents why I made the decision: it would have upset them too much. I just shook my head and kept saying that I would never set foot in the place again. From that moment on my father stopped talking to me. We didn't talk much anyway, but I'd just gone one step too far, I'd really disappointed him. Even now I can tell straight away when he wants to take me in his arms and tell me he loves me, but he holds back and slinks off without a word.

So for three months I worked at home, making sure I knew what happened in lessons and what books were on the syllabus. My mother gave me a hand on the quiet because my father didn't approve of my decision – and never would. In July I got a B in my Baccalaureate. I was so bloody proud that day! My mother cried, she was so happy when I rang and told her. That evening my father didn't speak any more than usual and we ate in silence because there was no question of celebrating anything whatsoever.

I can see now that I was very lucky. Was it really luck or motivation, an overriding desire to succeed? I know that sort of thing won't happen to me now, here in this amphitheatre. As a general rule, lecturers have too many students to remember all their names, to assess them individually and, therefore, to insult them. Here, you work for yourself alone.

I have several tutorials during the course of the day: translation work, language laboratory ... After five hours of lessons I head back towards my snug little nest where my boyfriend's waiting for me. It really has been a wonderful day, how could I be happier? I've got a boyfriend who loves me and I live with him in the centre of V, I'm at uni and, although I may not have much money, I'm young and healthy. What more could I ask for?

I get into the packed carriage on the Métro. I'm going to do well this year, I know it, I can feel it, I want it.

Chapter 4

Routine

4 October 2006

I GET HOME FROM lectures exhausted. I finish at eight o'clock on Wednesday evenings, then I have about forty-five minutes on the Métro. I'm tired from yesterday: I finished work at nine. On the journey I think about Manu, I can't wait to get back to him. I think about the meal he'll be putting together for me. Maybe he will have laid the table too, and lit a few candles.

When I get home this evening I know we'll also be talking about this month together. I'm worried about it because I know we've both got things on our minds that we're not saying. Our life together feels more and more like a flat-share. We only see each other in the evening and, when I get home, I gobble my supper so that I can get down to studying.

At first Manu was OK with it, sometimes pulling a bit of a face, but he would just say, 'Go on, go and work, you've got stuff to do.'

He would spend the evenings in front of the TV, hardly doing any work for uni. I would give him one last kiss and shut myself away in the bedroom.

Manu is one of that tiny proportion of people who have natural ability. He excels in his field but I've never really seen him work. Sometimes I'm jealous of him, of his intelligence and his ability to cope with things as they come along while I often have to study late into the night.

When he felt like going to bed Manu would come into the bedroom quietly: that would be my signal to go and work at the plastic table in the kitchen. Manu would already be sound asleep by the time I got into bed next to him, worn out. In the morning I would head off to uni or to work, depending on the day of the week.

Till now this routine has been fine for me because I've been with him. I earn about 400 euros from the telesales company. I handed over the eagerly awaited 300 euros for September's rent, pretending I didn't know he would blow it on evenings out with his mates, mostly spent smoking. I now haven't got much left for the rest of the month, nothing to have a bit of fun myself, do a bit of shopping or even go out with some girlfriends. Still, I don't want to ruin anything, we're too good together. I've never loved anyone as much as Manu.

But very soon, in less than a month, things have turned sour. Bored of having to spend every evening in front of the TV, Manu's started going out a lot, sometimes not getting home till the small hours. I put up with it at first because I didn't have anything better to offer him between my books and my job. I'm also happy to keep my independence and freedom but, just recently, time seems to be going so slowly for me. When I get home in the evening Manu's very often already gone out to meet his friends. I've got no way of knowing how long he'll be: sometimes all that's left of him is the tail end of a joint smouldering in an ashtray in the living room. He hardly devotes any time to me. Exhausted by my tough routine, I don't have the strength or the heart to stay up for him and I go to bed alone virtually every evening. I'm often tempted to lie down on the sofa and finish his joint, but I've never done it. Firstly, because he might be annoyed with me, but mostly because I wouldn't be able to work properly afterwards.

As time goes by Manu is getting more and more bitter and tight-fisted towards me. All his money is devoted to his evenings out and his spliffs. At first I couldn't come to terms with this so I convinced myself I was wrong, but the facts are clear to see: Manu can't bear what's turned into a boring flat-share, and he makes the point to me every day. I can't take life so lightly now, not like when I lived with my parents.

The worst thing is I get the distinct impression Manu looks down on me. He's always wearing new clothes – basically, he can afford all the things I can't. A rift has developed between us, and it's no longer just a financial rift, even if initially it was based on money. I can feel us getting a little further apart every day, and there's nothing I can do about it.

But this evening we had a date to have a special meal together. I've been asking to do this for a week because

I know we need to spend some time together. He gave in, and even offered to cook so all I need do is sit at the table. I've been getting ahead with my work all week on purpose. When I left uni I reapplied my make-up, using the window in the Métro as a mirror, so I'm pretty for him when I get home. Nothing much, just a bit of eyeliner.

As I step through the doorway I can tell something's not right. The apartment's far too quiet for Manu to be here. I've got to face the facts: he's not in. I have a look in the kitchen, trying to convince myself he's nipped out to buy some bread, but it's empty and there are no signs to suggest preparations for any meal. My tummy rumbles, I'm really hungry – I didn't have enough money to buy a sandwich at lunchtime so I stayed in the library and carried on working.

I sit down opposite the TV and cry. An hour goes by and Manu hasn't come home. So I try to do some work but I can't seem to concentrate. I can't even watch TV, my retina won't assimilate the sequence of images. Call a friend? What for? She'd only laugh at me and tell me boys are all the same and you can't trust them. Manu's not like that, Manu really loves me and cares about me.

But it's nearly midnight and Manu's still not back. I'm too proud to call him on his mobile and I haven't got any credit, anyway. I've smoked all my tobacco and the packet of roll-up papers is sitting uselessly on the table. Why's he doing this to me? Why me? Aren't I having a hard enough time as it is? It's only been a month and I've had it already, I'm exhausted the whole time trying to earn a measly bit of spare cash because I never actually get to see my own money.

All of a sudden there's a key turning in the lock. I hold my breath, I hadn't contemplated confronting Manu this evening. I quickly dry my tears with the back of my hand; I don't want to face him like this, my make-up must have run.

The next minute Manu's in the kitchen. I stare at him and he looks at me with his own eyes reddened by joints.

'How are you?' he says casually. 'Not working?'

I feel as if my body's going to explode. He can't be serious. He's stoned, I can tell that.

'What? Are you taking the piss? Where were you? Weren't we supposed to be having supper together this evening?'

I'm screaming, completely out of control. I'm so tired that, even while the words are spewing out of my mouth, I wonder where I'm getting the energy.

Manu looks away, he knows he's hurt me.

'Listen, Laura, I don't know what happened but I didn't want it to, I swear. I was here in the kitchen and I really was going to make you supper. I opened the fridge and saw you hadn't bought anything. It *was* your turn to do the shopping, wasn't it? Yes, it was your turn and you didn't do it.'

'So that's why, is it? So you decide to leave me here all evening crying just because of that? Is that how you want to punish me?'

'No, Laura, it's not just this shopping, it's everything. I know you haven't got any money, but we had an agreement about splitting expenses. On top of everything else, I got the gas bill today and that made things worse.'

He's looking me right in the eye and not raising his voice at all. However hard I try, I can't understand what he's saying, I can't see how he can dare to say all this when he knows I'm doing everything I can to help financially. I've always been embarrassed talking about money.

'And, like last time, it was me who had to go shopping because, otherwise, we'd have nothing to eat. I've had enough of giving in, I've had enough of you leaning on me the whole time. So I went out for a bit, to see a couple of friends, to cheer me up . . .'

I don't say anything, I can't really think what to add. Manu has reached the pinnacle of tightfistedness. He asks me for money for the rent, the shopping, the bills – which adds up to about 450 euros a month. I haven't got enough from my salary so I fill the gap with the bit of pocket money my mother gives me every month. It's not much: what little she can afford she gives to me. I stopped the contract on my phone a month ago, putting expenses from the apartment as a higher priority. On top of that, I work fifteen hours a week in the telesales place and twenty at uni, plus all the hours spent going over my coursework. He doesn't even work, and he spends the money his mother puts into his account for the rent on joints and clothes, and he's cashing in my share too. So, in fact, I don't see that I'm exploiting the situation, I pay my way and deserve my place in this apartment just as much as he does.

But, in spite of everything, I still adore him and, even now, I can't hate him. I'm too smitten to find any reply. I'm ashamed of myself for being so weak when it comes to a handsome face and devastating eyes.

Manu takes me in his arms at last, very gently, and I accept the hug. It's not a dramatic moment at all, it feels good being in his arms, that's all that matters. He loosens his hold a few minutes later, looks at me with those big dark eyes and suddenly says, 'Look, in future, to avoid this sort of situation, I think we should do our shopping separately, each do our own. It'll be easier for everyone and we won't have any more rows like this.'

I can't get over it. So everything that's happened this evening still isn't enough? He wants to make it even worse?

'What?'

'Yes, I really think it would be better for both of us. And with our different timetables we hardly ever eat together, and we don't like the same things, anyway.'

I still don't say anything – although that doesn't mean I'm not thinking. It's just, what is there to add? I'm not going to try convincing the biggest skinflint on earth. The very fact that he's bothered about this is enough for me to know I can't do anything to change him. He's tight-fisted and too spoilt, and he'll stay like that a good while yet. Meanwhile, he doesn't realise how much he's hurting me. My relationship is slowly falling apart.

I nod my head and force a smile, but we both know that something's wrong between us. Something to do with money. Perhaps something to do with different social backgrounds which, it turns out, he can't take. His mother often says I'm not good enough for him.

The next day, when I get home from work, he's made some room for me in the cupboard where we usually put tins.

Chapter 5

Hunger

26 October 2006

MY MOTHER DOESN'T TAKE her eyes off me as she hands me the plate of chicken. She hasn't stopped since the beginning of the meal. It's the *Toussaint* bank holiday and I'm spending two or three days with my parents; I haven't yet decided exactly how long I'm going to stay. We're sitting at the table, me, my mother, my silent father and my sister who won't stop talking.

'This chicken's good, isn't it, Laura?'

I know she's watching my every move. I drive my fork into the chunky thigh and, using my other hand, bring it up to my mouth and eat it like an ogre. I've got a huge appetite today, I'm so hungry. This supper is unquestionably the biggest feast I've had for a month.

'Yes, it's delicious,' I say, savouring it.

My sister is the only one making any conversation, and I'm the only one listening to her. I know the fact that I'm here is disturbing my father as he sits there thinking. He doesn't speak much, anyway, but when I'm here he becomes completely mute.

Our relationship has always been difficult; we've always loved each other, but in silence. My father's someone who commands respect. When he was twenty he left his native Spain to escape abject poverty and the dictatorship, and to try his chances in France. He was brought up in a very strict family which put a lot of store in respecting tradition. He's never lost that in-built coldness towards us, his daughters, particularly towards me, just like his own father with his children before him. I've always accepted it, because that's the way he works.

I know he loves me but he's never told me so, he's never put his feelings into words. I'm the oldest and I know I was a longed-for child. My parents really pampered me when I was tiny, but as I grew up and developed such a bond with my mother, my father retreated into silence, perhaps not knowing how to approach me. He probably thought it was abnormal and disrespectful that I kept my composure when he wanted to punish me. He's gradually shut himself away in his own world, which amounts to ignoring me. When I'm in the room he'll only talk to me if he really has to. I know my behaviour has disappointed him on several occasions; the lowest point was when I walked out on my last year of school.

My sister and I have always known that there was favouritism in the family: with me it was from my mother, and with her my father. But we can't do anything about it, and the fact that we've accepted this inescapable truth has meant there's been no resentment or jealousy between us.

I remember one time, when I was sixteen, leaving home for a month. The four of us were in the living room and I was looking at the sofa we were sitting on. It was a very old sofa covered in green fabric, and it's always been there. It was so old that, when I was still quite little, my mother decided to dye it dark red to hide the obvious wear and tear. As I sat listening to the television, I scratched at part of the armrest where the dye hadn't taken.

'Maybe we should dye it green again,' I said suddenly. 'It's been red for a long time now and could do with a new lease of life.'

'This sofa's never been green,' my father said without even looking at me. He spoke curtly and contemptuously as if I'd said the stupidest thing he'd ever heard.

'Of course it has, Dad. I can still remember when mum dyed it.'

I spent several minutes trying to prove it had and that I remembered it clearly. I even resorted to old photo albums to find proof of the case I was putting forward. When he saw me rummaging through the shelves my father flew into a furious, unjustified temper.

'Oh, you always have to be right, don't you? You always have to be so clever, Miss Know-it-all!'

He was bellowing, and my mother and sister stared at him, paralysed. I didn't move either, not sure what to do, still with a photo album in my hand.

'I've had just about enough of you, your attitude and your behaviour. You have no respect for other people, everything revolves around you, you're the centre of the universe. In fact, I can't stand you any more, you're just a . . . a little shit! That's it, a shit!'

He whispered the word hoarsely and went out to the kitchen. My sister cried out when she heard it. My father in all his glory, my father who doesn't mince his words. In spite of everything, it still sticks in my throat. I clenched my fists and started to run. My mother got up and tried to stop me as I grabbed for my bag. She cried and begged me not to go, and my sister hung on to my arm. My father didn't move a muscle from the kitchen.

'Mum, I can't, not any more. Look what he's like, I can't put up with it. I'm off.'

'But where to? How are you going to manage?'

'I'll find something.'

And I did. I lived with a friend, in her parents' house, for a month. They didn't really try to get to the bottom of it, just made a bit of room for me in their house – it was big enough. I went to school with my friend every morning, and called my mother once a week to let her know how I was.

I came back after a month; I didn't want to abuse the kindness extended by my friend and her parents. When I got home my father ignored me, as usual. He even went on ignoring me when the whole business had blown over. It hurt me terribly but I didn't know how to tell him or show him. I found out later he'd had tears in his eyes the day I left.

So the situation we're in now, this bank holiday, isn't at all unusual. My sister's talking to break the silence which she finds awkward but she eventually gets fed up with making all the conversation and stops. We finish our meal in silence.

My mother takes me to one side later in the evening. I know she's been wanting to talk to me ever since I got here.

'Laura, tell me something, are you eating all right?'

'Yes, Mum. You saw for yourself, I had three helpings of chicken this evening.'

'No, Laura, that's not what I mean. Do you eat properly when you're not here? Do you and Manu have enough to eat?'

She couldn't help but notice. I've lost a huge amount of weight in a month, since Manu and I have each had our own food cupboard. I weighed more than sixty kilos at the beginning of September, I was even a bit chubby, and I'm now down to fifty. I get in late and tired every evening and I often don't have time to cook anything because I have to study. I spend all day running from one place to another, from lectures to the library to work. I haven't got anything in my cupboard, anyway, apart from a half-used packet of pasta that's been there a couple of weeks. I often don't have lunch at uni, and by the end of the week a sandwich can feel like an extravagance. I've got so used to not eating, I don't really feel hungry any more. Well, almost.

Manu, on the other hand, often eats out with friends. I imagine he uses my share of the rent to splash out on good food while I'm buried in my books. Apart from that, we get on pretty well, no real rows. Mind you, that's no surprise because we hardly ever see each other. But I still love him with all my might ... Even when I open his food cupboard and drool with longing at his tins of pâté and his jars of pesto which would make my pasta so much more appetising.

One time I took a slice of his Parma ham, thinking he wouldn't notice. Just my luck, he must have counted them because he noticed the theft straight away. I apologised at length, explaining that I was just hungry and would buy him some more, which I did the next day, blowing my five-euro note which was supposed to last me three days. I could have laboured the point and just given him back one slice – perhaps he would have realised how ridiculous he was being. But I don't want to play his games, it's not my thing.

I definitely can't tell my mother all this. She'd go mad and call Manu every name under the sun. She'd make me come home, which is completely out of the question.

'Don't worry, Mum, everything's fine.'

'You would tell me if something was wrong, wouldn't you?'

'Of course I would, Mum. Don't fuss.'

She gives me a long look so I have plenty of time to see how sceptical she is. She doesn't believe me, but she can't do anything if I don't tell her the truth.

Two days later when I leave my parents' house, my mother gives me a whole bag full of provisions; she's put everything she can lay her hands on in there. She gives me a wink as she hands it to me.

'Have a good trip, my darling, take care.'

My father just waves at me and doesn't kiss me. We haven't kissed for years now.

Chapter 6

Shame

16 November 2006

I'M OUTSIDE THE STUDENT welfare offices hesitating to go in. I'm not so sure I want to go there now. I'm hanging back slightly, not quite opposite the door.

It's November and the weather's freezing. My weight loss has really accelerated in the last couple of months; it's as if I can feel the cold going right through me and it's never done that before. And that's even though I made a point of putting on lots of layers of clothes this morning. Since I've been this thin I'm cold the whole time. I shake all over, even in my insides: in lessons, at work, at home.

Winter is coming on in leaps and bounds and we still haven't put the heating on in the apartment. At least, *I* don't want to put it on. Manu sets it going the minute he gets in before installing himself on the sofa like the lord of the manor. I wait for him to go out and switch it off straight away. I've been doing this ever since I've been paying my share of the bills. Electricity, water and heating, it all it adds up to quite a lot. Manu couldn't care less because he's not the one who has to budget for these expenses. So he hikes up the heating while I secretly keep lowering it because I can't bring myself to ask him this favour.

At first I did my studying in normal clothes but I quickly realised that sitting still for several hours without moving made me feel so cold I might as well have been outside. So now, when I'm working, I put on quite an outfit: a huge scarf knitted by my mother, a sports fleece and thick socks that come up to my knees. Manu laughed the first time he saw me like that and I did too when I saw myself in the mirror. For a couple of seconds. Because there's nothing funny about the situation if you think about it. In the end I got used to this excess weight on my frail shoulders – the money saved helped. I'd rather look as if I'm off mountaineering than have to pay fifty euros on an avoidable bill.

I put as much money as I can aside and never buy anything non-essential. It goes without saying I gave up clothes shopping long ago. Mainly, because I don't have time and, anyway, what would be the point of drooling over something I'll never have? So I avoid temptation and I'm careful to avoid window shopping. I've finally got it into my head that I'll never wear the latest fashion. Of course sometimes I could just die for a pair of new-cut jeans, one of those belted jackets and a pair of astronomically priced shoes like my friends at uni wear. All I can do is look, until it becomes embarrassing and I have to sigh and get back to what I'm doing. I'd like to be strong enough to say that I hate any sort of consumer culture and find it repulsive, but let's be honest: is there anyone who *never* wishes for anything and doesn't give in to well-marketed temptations? I'm young and there's advertising everywhere – I'd be easy prey if I had any money.

I envy the girls around me in lectures. Looking fresh and rested, some of them have never had to work to survive financially. Their parents earn plenty of money to support them. Sometimes they must go shopping with their mothers and hint that they like something with a well-practised pout, to which their mothers reply by taking out a credit card. I can't resent them for it, I'd do the same without a second thought. I just envy them their peace of mind when I'm the one shaking each time I see a ticket inspector on the Métro, and constantly asking myself how I'm going to cope at the end of the month. I quake when Manu casually asks me for my share of the rent too. Am I the only one going through this? I'm so ashamed of the situation I can't talk to my fellow students about it. How could they understand? So I politely decline their invitations to join them for lunch and shut myself away with the only free thing left: studying.

None of this would really be a problem if I could get enough to eat. The state of my food cupboard is still just as pathetic, and the things my mother gave me didn't last long. Pasta, pasta and more pasta. When the time comes to make a meal, I look at it and feel it's sneering at me, pointing out that this evening – yet again – I can't do better than that. In the early days I had it with tins of tomato sauce, but indigestion problems during the night have turned me off that, and the very thought of pasta swimming in cheap sauce turns my stomach. A dab of butter's not so bad after all.

There's also a pot of Nutella, my little taste of happiness. I never eat more than a spoonful at a time, so I can keep it as long as possible. It's there to comfort me when I open the cupboard.

I've spent so long feeling hungry I've stopped eating. That was how I realised that, after a while, hunger disappears and the human life cycle just carries on of its own accord. After a few days of this regime I don't really feel any pain. I've got into the habit of not having lunch and doing several consecutive days at uni with nothing in my stomach. Sometimes it makes strange noises during lectures, but I'm so used to them that I hardly hear them any more.

One girl in my class turned round and gave me a chocolate bar and joked kindly, 'Here, have something to eat, all we can hear round here's your stomach gurgling!'

I was very ashamed and whispered a thank you, trying to pretend I thought she was being very amusing, but I didn't find it funny at all. I savoured that chocolate bar, slowly and silently. If I'd been somewhere else I would have gobbled it down in a matter of seconds because I wanted it so badly. I controlled myself, with dignity, but

I did make sure I got every last shard that fell on my notes, dabbing them with my finger. I could easily have eaten another one.

In the evening, if I've got the time or the energy to eat when I get home from uni or from work, I have a bowl of rice pudding. And if I need to lift my spirits, a spoonful of Nutella at the end of my 'meal'. It may seem pathetic but that chocolate has a calming effect. I lick the spoon clean to get the maximum amount of taste, right to the end. I feel as if I work better afterwards.

Then, towards the end of one morning, the thing that was bound to happen happened. I collapsed right in the middle of a lesson. I'd pushed my luck so far I didn't realise I'd gone beyond my own body's limits. People got into quite a state but I came to very quickly and got back to work. Some of them kept saying I should go and see the campus nurse, which I politely refused to do. No need for medics to tell me what's wrong with me: I'm suffering from a deficiency of money.

That was the day I decided to go to the welfare office to find a solution, some financial help. This lack of money is affecting my health and I'm not prepared to accept that state of affairs. I hate the fact I have to work so hard just to eat, and to eat so I can carry on working. But now that I'm outside the building I haven't got the strength to go in. I would never have guessed I could end up here for this. I know a lot of students come here to ask for help, but it's not in my nature. For me, coming here is tantamount to failure: I haven't managed to cope on my own. But I've got to face the facts. I can't do this by myself, I need a bit of help from somewhere. This permanent hunger can't go on any longer.

So I go inside and wait meekly at reception. A woman sees me half an hour later having dealt with a great crowd of students at breakneck speed. In her office I beat about the bush before admitting, 'OK, I've come to see you because I've got big financial problems and I wondered whether I could get any kind of help from your organisation.'

Then it all starts coming out, and I describe my life, the lack of money, Manu and the rent, the rushing to and from work, the gap getting bigger every day. While I'm talking I watch her reaction: she's listening attentively and seems concerned by what I'm telling her. She's young, in her thirties, she must remember her own time as an impoverished student.

After a good fifteen minutes of explanations I finally stop talking but, instead of answering, all she does to fill the silence is give a little cough.

'All I can offer at this moment in time,' she says eventually, 'are some vouchers so you can eat in the welfare office. They're good value, each meal is less than three euros!'

I do some quick mental arithmetic. I can't spend nearly fifteen euros a week on just one meal a day. I came here in the hopes of being offered significant reductions so that I can eat lunch *and* supper.

'It's just . . . that would add up to so much by the end of the week. I wondered whether you had any other possibilities.'

'In your circumstances, I can think of only one way to avoid spending money on food: the local soup kitchen for the homeless.'

She says it slowly, very gently, conscious of the psychological impact her words will have on me. And they do. I open my eyes wide and stare at her. There, in one sentence, is my position on the social scale: at the very bottom. So far down I can't pay for my own meals, so low I'm being offered food meant for the homeless. I must be dreaming, I can't believe she's being serious. But she's still looking at me, her eyes wide with understanding.

I mumble a vague 'Thank you' and ask where I have to go to find the soup kitchen. She takes a piece of paper and jots down an address . . . in beautiful handwriting – perhaps she's making an effort to prove she's touched by my lowly situation. I say my goodbyes quickly, desperate to get this over with. She shakes my hand warmly in the corridor before shrieking, 'Next.'

I confront the November cold back outside the building and, clutching the piece of paper, walk off quickly to keep warm. I won't go, no way. I can't make up my mind to go to a place like that; I tell myself I don't need it all that badly, when all's said and done. I would almost feel I was 'stealing' the food from those poor people who really don't have anything. But most of all I can't reconcile myself with them, the homeless. I've got a roof over my head, a job, my studies. No, that's it, my pasta suits me just fine, really, I'll make do with it. After all, I'm not the first . . . or the last.

Chapter 7

The End

9 December 2006

IN EVERY LIFE there comes a night when we grow up too quickly. Nothing will ever be the same again. Goodbye to innocence. One of those mournful nights when it hurts to take stock of the situation. As it happens, mine is financial. No money, bills vying for attention and rent to pay. Sitting in the dark, leaning back against the chair in front of Manu's computer, I'm barely in control of my finger as it frenetically manipulates the mouse in search of a solution. A site full of ads, then another. A small window catches my eye; it's almost hidden at the bottom of the page, trying to be discreet, and says 'For Adults Only'. There are two categories of listings: money-making or non-money-making. I'm immediately tempted to choose the second, as if trying to justify my actions to someone . . . but the room's empty, I'm on my own. Let's be honest, money's still very much my main reason for being on this site. *Just out of curiosity*, I tell myself, knowing full well I've already stepped over the limit. Without any vetting, I click on the window (adults only, yeah right!). In the 'key words' box, I put that I'm a student and give the name of the city.

An endless list of requests then appears and I scroll through it with my mouse. Is it really possible and so easy? I skim through the ads which, at a quick glance, are all alike. The same words keep cropping up: 'young girl', 'intimacy', 'meet up', 'seeking'. I'm seeking too: money, and quickly. The men here – stupidly categorised under the dubious alibi of 'massage' – are on average well into their fifties. Older than my own father. *Daddy, if you only knew* . . . The main difference is they've got cash, lots of it, and they seem prepared to spend it to feed a fantasy that I'm potentially in a position to satisfy. The rates, if they're mentioned at all, are in hundreds of euros per hour. Can that be right? All these figures soon aggravate my longing to have some money of my own. I can already see myself with all that loot in my battered purse – it would be spilling out in every direction! They also talk about several hours spent together. What does one afternoon matter in a lifetime! I would have thought that, if you really need the money, it wouldn't mean a lot. Perhaps this is my solution, the one I've been looking for. A bit of comfort, and soon.

Still, I've made do without comfort until now, and quite well actually. My parents' council flat until I was eighteen, the cheapest simplest clothes, roll-up cigarettes

– that was plenty for me. Until now. Of course I was envious sometimes, like everyone else, but I'd never really been materialistic . . . Perhaps I couldn't afford to be. Never two coins to rub together, always dodging fares on public transport, a tolerable life. Occasionally awkward, often embarrassing when a bill came along, but you muddle through. I try to tell myself these 'massages' would mean I could easily afford to have choices. I don't realise that the exact opposite is happening: I'll never have a choice again.

There in the darkness – so often at the root of irrational actions – I become sharply alert until my senses seem to be boiling. First, my eyesight, so painful and constantly there: the sight of bills pilling up unopened, abandoned on the humble piece of furniture in the living room that I use as a bookcase; the sight of money offered by my few friends to pay for my coffee at the local bistro for the umpteenth time. A hypothesis begins to emerge, and one that may have been lying dormant all these years: with some cash I'd not only be able to study the whole time, but I'd actually like myself a bit more.

My mind's racing. My whole body's clamouring for all these possibilities, I can almost feel them with the tips of my fingers. All I have to do is click on the mouse, that's all, just a tiny bit of pressure. My hand refuses to be controlled, it's motivated by this dark longing – so taboo and, paradoxically, so dazzlingly exciting. My arms, my head, the whole of me knows that there, at the end of my arm, is an answer, however controversial it may be, a way to sort everything out, at least for now. Every part of me gangs up against the feeble voice of reason in my head, they just want to get it over with. Who cares about afterwards, we'll see about that later.

I've suddenly been gripped by a sort of frenzy, it's already too late. All I need do is look back at those messages and I'm completely in their hands. *Don't think, Laura, just type out these fucking messages and you'll get out of all the shit you're in – it's the only way out and you know it.* I mustn't back away out of fear. I've been offered a chance, I need to jump at it. My go-getting attitude can no longer see the difference between good and bad, it wants a way out more than anything, whatever the cost. From that moment on a sort of schizophrenia takes over. I've become two different people since seeing the ads: there's the Laura who's perfectly aware she's playing with fire and the Laura desperate for money. A ridiculous sense of defiance comes into the mix: I can do this, I'll prove it to myself. So I type, I type away on my keyboard as if each letter pressed could eradicate the gaping hole inside me getting bigger every day. I believed I was in control of my faculties as I set out on the wrong path, now I feel invincible just at the thought of this money.

Manu's not here, make the most of it. Still, I glance at the time and at the front door, just in case. He's still with his friends at the moment, he won't be back straight away.

I type quickly, not stopping to think, to avoid imagining the world I'm straying into. I'm falling: yes, it only took five minutes for me to fall. An hour later my hands stop, satisfied. I've sent about forty replies in my manic enthusiasm. But what does forty mean? These people don't really exist yet. The hazy image of them conjured by their words doesn't mean anything to me. The feeling that it's all just a dream never actually went away. The whole time my fingers tinkered on the keyboard I was very careful not to think about what I was doing. To put a stop to my daydreaming, I snap the laptop shut and go out to get some air.

Nightfall was all it took. In the first hour of darkness, the idea of loneliness and longing for human company came to mind, like an echo of what I need myself. In a way we're the same, them and me; we all need something. Maybe I wasn't actually dreaming. My mailbox is already showing the consequences of my actions – actions that are even now out of my control, even in the safety of my own home. I answered . . . lost in a frenzy of need, desperate to find this fucking money, and now I'm face to face with my own stupidity. So the thought of a female student really does it for the older man, I've got proof of that now. It seems they've all found what they were looking for; they want their fantasies to be made a reality, and I mine.

You always remember the first message. Mine is from Joe, an unusual name in France but the one he uses to sign off his emails to me. Joe, usually known as Joseph. It seemed obvious to him to use a pseudonym: on the one hand, it makes him seem younger and more in touch to his potential 'collaborators in pleasure', on the other, it avoids exposing his true identity. Does he too become two people as it gets dark at night and he feels the urge rising in him? I didn't try giving myself a pseudonym. Too inexperienced, too new, I didn't even think about it. I stupidly believe Laura will always be Laura, whatever happens.

Young 50-year-old man seeks occasional masseuse. Students welcome.

His message is oddly polite but, reading between the lines, you can feel him sweating with longing. He asks me whether I have any taboos . . . his words begging that I won't, implying the pay will be even better. He hasn't asked for a photo but has sent me one. He's fifty-seven. That gives you an idea of what he might look like. Reality hits me now, tough and uncompromising, forcing me to realise what I'm doing.

As I read his message I really feel like a little child for the first time in my life, and I'm someone who's always been old for her years. This is a mature man, three times my age. He's talking about well thought-out fantasies that have obviously been buried deep but never quashed. He's looking for a naive girl, probably picturing her in a pleated skirt with knee socks, sucking on a strawberry-flavoured lollipop. Then he switches off his computer because his wife's walked into the room and asked him to come and have supper with her and their daughter. And during the meal he acts as if nothing's happened because he's been hiding all this from them for years now.

He might have a quick look at his daughter – who's older than the girl in the short kilt – and think how pretty she is and how promising her future. When she asks him to pass her something he does it happily, with a smile. At night, on a good day, he makes love to his wife – politely, taking his time, controlling himself so she has time to enjoy it. Because he loves her. Because he loves both of them, from the bottom of his heart.

The question of rates is elaborated on, and I swindle myself without any help from him. With the anonymity of the net, there are so many lies and they're so easy to hide that I've slipped effortlessly into the guise of a professional prostitute who's been around the block and can't be tricked. But when I have to talk about money, I put my foot in it. My instant reaction was to ask for hundreds and thousands but I thought that wouldn't be realistic. With time, I'll realise you won't lose anything by daring to raise the stakes, even if it means renegotiating if there's too much resistance.

These men imagine – and in my case, I have to admit, quite rightly – that if a girl asks a lot then she must be worth it. An astronomical sum often means they can expect a pleasant surprise: perhaps a really stunning girl whose body alone means she can raise her prices. Getting what you pay for, so to speak. They probably think these are girls who like sex, who keep asking for more, coquettish young students who want mature men to take control of their monotonous sex lives, to make a change from the brainless pretty boys their own age.

My inexperience means I ask for a hundred euros an hour, matching what I'd seen in other ads. Our friend Joe seems delighted – he most likely wasn't expecting that sort of sum. It was probably at that point that he realised he was dealing with a first-timer. I'm sure he won't have wasted any time imagining scenarios, pushing the boundaries that a 'pro' would normally impose.

We arrange to meet up after a brief exchange of emails which I pretended to get involved in. We're meeting in three days, in a hotel near the station. He'll be wearing a red polo shirt so I can recognise him because, although I've got his photo, he doesn't want to miss me, to make the trip for nothing. He makes a real point of saying he doesn't live in the city, and would be very disappointed if I wasn't there after he's come all this way. Talking to me like a little girl, like giving a child a warning when you know she's going to do something silly.

I say 'yes' straight away, to get the subject out of my mind as quickly as possible. Even so, the details are already falling into place. A patchwork is gradually being pieced together inside my head. In my mind's eye, I think of his face and connect it to the body of a man in his sixties, wearing a red polo shirt. I place this combination outside a crumby hotel on the street that goes down to the station, a street with quite a reputation for prostitution and drug trafficking.

Once I've closed the computer down and extinguished the last embers of my imaginings, I go back to my humdrum little life in a flash. Manu still isn't here, the prick, so I decide to immerse myself in a Spanish translation exercise. But I can't seem to concentrate. After a few minutes' thinking, I manage to persuade myself not to go and meet Joe, on any account. I've played with fire, a bit, and even burnt my fingers but I've absolutely no intention of really going. Joe will stand outside that hotel all alone, I'll still be at home.

Still, that stupid figure keeps coming to mind: a hundred euros an hour. Three days to wait. To wait for what? I've decided not to go, so why have I got it into my head that I should respect the agreement I made with this stranger? I won't go, that's it, end of story. My thoughts seesaw backwards and forwards, between what I should do and what I need, very careful to avoid my poor young heart, which doesn't have any part in all this.

I look at my food cupboard, my empty food cupboard. Stupidly, I have a quick look at my bills on the bookcase. I've got a headache. I snap my translation book shut.

Once, just once.

Chapter 8

The Mug

12 December 2006

I T'S ONLY THREE DAYS since our exchange of emails. And, actually, that's not a bad thing. At least it means I haven't had time to think about what I'm doing . . . and I need the money too badly. We've agreed to meet at two o'clock, for an hour at a cost of a hundred euros. Just an hour, before I go off to work at the telesales company. Right up to the last minute I don't know whether I'm really going to go. But the hole in my pocket kind of spurs me on.

I'm not really sure how or why, but here I am heading towards that wretched street, walking like someone going to a meeting they haven't put in their diary but still can't forget. I've tried hard to pretend I really don't care about this meeting by putting on a boring pair of jeans and a jacket. But under these supposedly normal clothes – in case I bump into someone on the way – no one would guess I'm wearing stockings, which are chafing slightly. It made me laugh when I put them on, I feel a bit ridiculous in them. I even shaved in the shower this morning. Obviously, I do that pretty often, specially since I've been living with Manu, but this time I made a real effort, going back over my knees and ankles several times. A very tricky place, ankles. The reason I did this so carefully isn't absolutely clear yet.

On my way I realise I haven't prepared an explanation in case I meet someone in the street. It doesn't matter that much, anyway, I'm a good liar, I'll come up with something. When I get close to the station I do start hurrying though. The sooner I get there, the sooner it'll be over.

I go through the rules I want to stick to inside my head, methodically: once, just once. I should have smoked a joint before leaving. Yes, that's right, why didn't I think of it? I'd have been much more chilled out, more relaxed, I might even have found the whole thing amusing. Might.

Weirdly, I want to take a few precautions, things I think are important: I won't show myself first, I'll wait till he gets here. Deep down, I still feel as if this is some kind of joke. Stationed outside the appointed hotel, I wait in the chill December air, watching passers-by, almost wanting Joe to turn up just so I don't have to go on enduring this icy wind. Joe, the rough sketch who will become a reality in a few moments' time.

Masses of perfectly logical questions mill around my mind. He said he'd booked a room – did he give his real name at reception? I didn't say anything when he suggested coming here but I think it's such a grim choice. He must test out all his new conquests here and, if they deserve it, he makes their day by taking them to more salubrious places after that. But, actually, if all he wants is sex, why make such a fuss about it? If that's what it is, then he doesn't need much else.

Just before the agreed time, an older looking man stops outside the building and looks around casually, quite naturally. 'Older', that's what people say when they want to be polite and avoid saying plain 'old'. So, basically, he's old. I would never have thought I'd end up sleeping with a man that age.

He doesn't look anything like the photo. Despite the younger, sporty image he's gone for, he certainly looks his age. He's wearing a red checked shirt, tracksuit bottoms and trainers; with greying hair to match his years. The middle of his face is adorned by a large moustache, still brown in colour. Not very stylish but at least he looks clean. Someone I certainly wouldn't have looked at twice in the street, but he's not repellent either. To think I'm going to see him naked! To think he'll want to touch me! I'm shivering with disgust at the thought. Perhaps because I was expecting much worse, I jump out from my hiding place and cross the street to join him. I also think I'm already forcing myself to switch off my mind.

He sees me coming and his expression changes. I couldn't say whether it's for the better or the worse. We give each other a hasty peck on each cheek, obviously both quite tense. But he's suddenly relaxing and introduces himself very politely, in a gentle voice. My God, he's so old! Oh yes, he's all of fifty-seven now.

'Hello, Laura,' he says, watching me intently.

'Hello, Joe,' I say, not knowing what else to add.

I can't help looking him up and down, completely unashamedly. I don't feel any particular empathy for him, more like loathing, to be honest. I'm struck by his accent and it makes me want to inspect him carefully – he's got boring country bumpkin written all over him. His intonation, the way he puts a lilt at the end of each sentence . . . he's a perfect example of a country boy sent off to make a career in the 'big city' but never quite shaking off his origins. Right now, I'm wondering whether he really will pay me. Given his basic – not to say downright cheap – clothes, I have every right to be worrying about it.

The way he carries himself betrays an element of routine: this obviously isn't the first time. He appears to be delighted with how I look, and I pretend not to notice that he's ogling me with his crinkly old eyes. I'm like a gift from the gods for him: what more could he ask? A student, giving her body for the first time and, what's more, for a ridiculously low price. He's quivering with pleasure in anticipation and is privately congratulating himself for his excellent choice.

As for me, I'm glancing round frantically; I've been filled with insurmountable fear ever since we met up. I desperately want to get inside because there's only one thing I'm worried about at the moment and that's being recognised. He must have gathered that from the tension on my face, because he's leading the way. He must have gathered lots of things, seeing me there on the pavement for the first time.

I sneak through the main entrance behind him. From the way he's behaving I can tell he knows the ropes.

I walk behind him politely, as if trying to hide. I decide I don't want to see the look on the receptionist's face – he's no fool, he knows exactly what's going on and that this room hasn't been booked in the middle of the afternoon for a couple of tourists who've just got off a train and are tired from their journey.

I've been so busy hiding myself I didn't notice the policemen straight away. Joe didn't slow down or turn a hair at the sight of them. Basically, he didn't do anything to give me the nod. But they really are there: two of them in their distinctive *képis*, chatting by the reception desk. Now that I'm face to face with them I'd be happier with the accusing stare of the stranger at the desk.

Still, it suddenly dawns on me that the receptionist couldn't matter less, and that what might happen next could have much more impact on my life. Policemen can land you in prison.

Once I'm level with them, I look away, panicking. A horribly familiar feeling of heat – a physical warning of imminent danger – is spreading through my stomach and tormenting my insides. This is it, it's over almost before it's begun. This is it, I'm not yet twenty and I'm going to be caught out at some pitiful game because I didn't gauge the consequences properly. I keep walking while my imagination plays out a sequence worthy of a Hollywood film: I can see myself down at the station with a dazzling white light trained on my face, and handcuffs on my wrists, as I sit on a metal chair protesting my innocence. And my parents are summoned to my local police station, my mother in tears obviously, and my father not even looking at me because I've sullied the family name. What a nightmare!

I keep going, sure that any moment one of the policemen is going to stop me. My feet keep treading one ahead of the other, in spite of everything, following the man responsible for this whole business, for my future life as a convict. But what about him? Joe doesn't seem in the least bothered about what's going on around us. Fuck it, do something, the cops are going to nab us!

I don't cry out though. I'm so paralysed that no sound comes from my mouth at all. Hang on a minute: if the brute isn't batting an eyelid, then maybe he's in on it too. Could he be a plain clothes policeman? Oh, I've really been had . . .

I'm still busy hating myself, along with the whole rest of the world, when I realise we're already in the lift. He hasn't even suggested going separate ways and meeting up in the room, which would have betrayed a bit of perfectly logical concern. In fact, he couldn't give a monkey's about the cops. I get an explanation a few minutes later because something incredible happens: nothing. Absolutely bugger all. The policemen saw us, of course they did, we brushed right past them. Still, nothing's happened.

Instead, we've carried on with our journey in the lift in silence, with him probably already fantasising about what he's going to do once we get up there; and me still petrified, not yet recovered from the head-on impact with the law. When we get up to our floor he goes over to the room without a moment's hesitation – he must know the hotel like the back of his hand.

The first thing I notice are those hideous faded green curtains drawn across both windows. Fucking ugly décor! What sort of person has such bad taste to put curtains like that in a room like this? The rest is pretty basic. Quite big but only with the bare essentials: a bed and matching bedside tables, a desk up against the wall with a phone. It's a good thing I've spotted that straight away; I could lunge for it if Joe gets violent. The carpet's boring, very dark blue, nearly black, I can't be quite sure.

A snapping turn of a key brings me back to reality. Joe has locked us in. No way! We still haven't said a word to each other, except for standard introductions.

'No, the door stays unlocked,' I say.

What a nerve! I've hardly said the words before realising just how curt I sounded. Can you do that to a man you're supposed to be giving yourself to completely? I have absolutely no idea right now. It's the real Laura talking, the one who speaks her mind. He's pulling a bit of a face, just for a moment but long enough for me to see it.

'If you like. It was just so we could be left alone.'

He's not arguing about it and respects my request. Perhaps this won't be all that hard after all.

I'm so wound up and uneasy I can't stop moving, walking aimlessly backwards and forwards between the few pieces of furniture as if trying to offload my stress.

'Are you feeling OK?' he asks.

I'm so obviously tense that the old boy feels he has to ask how I am.

'Yes, I'm fine,' I say quickly to get the pointless conversation over with.

'So, you're a student, are you? A student of what? How old are you, actually?'

I can't bring myself to answer. I'm in too much of a state and too busy looking at him. He's fairly athletic looking and, apart from the pukey shirt, the rest is pretty acceptable. In a way I'm impressed by how old he is.

He continues to ask me a couple of boring questions, and I'm no more forthcoming with them, more out of awkwardness than bad manners.

I turn round and see those ugly curtains again. Why am I so obsessed with them? Everything about them is repulsive. They're sneering at me with that fabric no one's ever washed. I know that they only bother me this much because they're a reflection of my ugly, miserable situation.

He comes across the room carrying a small brown case I hadn't noticed till now. A real businessman's briefcase. He puts it gently down on the bed and starts to work the combination lock. Such an incongruous scene: just try to picture this bloke playing the great professional in his stupid lumberjack shirt!

What's he actually hiding in there? I have a quick enquiring look. At the moment I'm expecting him to take out all sorts of medical equipment, tools and utensils to butcher me. Or perhaps just one little gadget to add a bit of spice to our activities. I'm suddenly very worried about what he might want to get up to; after all, I don't know him from Adam.

The briefcase is lying open on the bed. For a moment I think I'm in a Tarantino film and, as I move closer to see what's inside it, I even picture wodges of banknotes. Instead it's just a boring letter which Joe hands to me.

'What do you want me to do? Read here in front of you?'

Without a word, he nods to mean yes. He's not exactly eccentric but is desperately trying to create something enigmatic in the situation, that's blindingly obvious. Well, I have to admit it's working. Disconcerted, I pick up the piece of paper. The writing is neat and it's clear from the start he's chosen his words carefully.

Dear Laura,

First of all, I'm pleased with your punctuality and would like to thank you for it.

What an idiot! Did he write a different letter in case I was late?

We're going to play a game together today. I'd like you to read my letter all the way through and do what it says as you go along. First of all, I want you to take all your clothes off.

Time seems to have mutated into a vast embarrassed silence. Joe isn't saying anything, just standing with his arms crossed. A proper job interview. If I pass the nudity test, I'm bound to be offered the job.

I slowly put the letter down on the edge of the bed. Without thinking I take off my top and, not waiting for any reaction from him, slide my jeans down over my thighs. I lower myself in what I hope is a slightly languid movement to get them right off.

He can't take his eyes off me, his mouth is gaping. I can see the beginnings of an erection beneath his jogging pants.

My bra, cotton knickers and stockings are now the only things hiding my anatomy. I stand in front of him with my hands behind my back, offering him all this intimacy. I'm the child-woman, Nabokov's Lolita, and he loves it. I'm completely disconnected from reality. This is like torture for me but I dispel it with a giggle. I've got so many complexes about my body, even though it's so slim now, and I'm genuinely finding this situation confusing. He doesn't move and hasn't said anything for quarter of an hour.

He takes a deep breath and begins to open his lips. Go on, say something.

'Wow!' he manages to exclaim quickly.

And that's it. One exclamation. No one could understand how I suddenly feel. All at once my body is filled with hope and a sort of happiness. With just one word and in a fraction of a second, this man I've never met before has succeeded where dozens of others have failed:

making me realise my body's attractive. Why did it have to be him? I can't answer that, it's just inexplicable. All I know is that it's the first time I've heard and accepted a compliment. That's when I start thinking of him as a man and not some great creep who wants to put his mitts all over me. He must have seen strings and strings of girls but he can still be impressed.

We give each other a knowing smile and something oddly like trust is reached between us.

'This is exactly the sort of reason I don't like "professionals". They can't have that innocent look you've got.'

I don't really know how to take this comment. Does he already think of me as a prostitute? Does it just take a couple of tricks to warrant that label?

He's tilted his chin towards the letter again for me to carry on reading. I do as I'm told.

Now I want you to go and have a shower. I'll have one after you. I'm very happy you're here and we're spending this time together.

I skim through to the end of the letter. I mean, the rest is obvious: once I'm naked and have had my shower it's not like we're going to launch into a fiendish game of Scrabble.

Thank you, Laura, for coming here today. I'm so happy to have met you and I do hope we'll see each other again soon. You seem like a nice person.

A nice person? How can he know? Am I a nice person because I've agreed to stand in front of him in my underwear to get the money I need? The letter ends with a whole blah blah blah of boring stuff he must have felt he had to write to ease his conscience and make me trust him. Still, his words betray a kindness I would never have imagined. This meeting isn't going as I thought it would. There I was thinking it would be an hour of blanking out my mind, putting my thoughts to one side, but now I can't help thinking about this man.

I take off the few scraps of fabric left on me and head meekly for the bathroom.

When I've closed the door I confront the mirror in that tiny room. Despite my best efforts, I can't avoid my reflection. Standing there naked in front of that mirror, I'm very tempted to succumb to self-pity. Once again I feel disconnected from this 'session' because I've come face to face with myself, with what I'm doing. I've never really looked at myself so closely and so carefully. I'm oddly proud of my body since Joe's exclamation and I start to scrutinise myself. I've never much liked my tummy but I look at it differently now. Somewhere deep inside me there's a voice trying to bring me back to my senses. Shit, I'm completely losing the plot, torn between two different feelings.

The fact that I have to shower creates a break in the proceedings, a break that forces me to think long and hard. I turn on the water and adjust the pressure to try to stop the whirring in my head.

It may seem incongruous but I'm smiling. Yes, smiling because I suddenly think I look good. I've gone back to childhood and that compliment from this man who's older than my own father has made me happy as a child being praised by her grandfather.

The water flows gently over my body and I lather it frenetically with the cheap soap graciously provided by the hotel. There isn't any need to scrub so hard, he hasn't touched me yet. But I carry on rubbing even harder, as if wanting to tear my skin. Perhaps I'm washing away this situation, the man himself, the room, his compliments, the green curtains.

Once I'm clean I grab a towel to dry myself and secure it expertly between my breasts, panicking at the thought of him coming into the bathroom. I hesitate for a moment. I don't know whether I'm supposed to go out naked or not. While I'm wondering about this I realise that, sooner or later, I'll be naked in front of him. It might just as well be me who decides. I grasp the knot between my breasts and undo it. The towel falls limply to the floor with a muffled sound.

When I open the door Joe is on the bed in his boxer shorts. I can see his torso for the first time. No surprises there. He certainly is fifty-seven, with white hairs and a slight paunch.

'You really turn me on, you know,' he says with a sigh.

Yes, I'm sure I do.

'Right, this is what's going to happen,' he says, then pauses before adding calmly, 'I love role playing. I have a lot of fantasies about it.'

Noticing my slightly disconcerted expression, he's quick to explain what he means.

'Now I want you to leave the room and wait in the corridor for a moment, then knock on the door twice. When I tell you to come in, you'll come in and do as I tell you.'

'What, you mean like this? Completely naked?'

'Yes, like that, completely naked.'

You wouldn't like a hundred euros into the bargain, by any chance! The way things are going I'm going to end up paying him. The fantasy of the naked girl knocking at the door is too much. What would happen if someone saw me? I'm feeling lost now.

'No.'

'What do you mean no? Why not?'

'No.'

'Am I allowed to know why?'

His expression's changed suddenly. I can tell from the tone of his voice that my refusal has just shattered the titillating image he was putting together. He knows I can put the dampers on his lewd inventions and, even though I am trapped and perfectly polite, he's not prepared to accept that.

I'm frightened now: I've broken his rules. I realise he won't give up on the goal he's set if I don't follow the instructions.

'Because this is difficult for me. Getting undressed in front of you was already a huge step. I don't know, I'm not sure now I can go any further. You're rushing things.'

Before coming I didn't think I'd have to talk to him so much. I'm prepared to give him my body so he can do what he wants with it while I close my eyes to get through the hour, but I don't want to have to act so much. Dead dog for an hour, maybe, but not an actress.

My response was genuine and after a while his expression softens. But deep in his eyes I can tell he won't give up.

'Listen, I do understand, but –' bingo, there's the 'but' '– don't be frightened, trust me, everything'll be fine. All you have to go is go out of the room for a moment and knock on the door . . .'

I obey him as quickly as possible yet again; the sooner I do this the sooner I'll get my hands on his money. My money. I already think of it as mine, otherwise I wouldn't be able to carry on.

So I go over to the door and, naked as I am, step outside – not without a quick glance round first. What a ridiculous situation! Humiliating even. If Manu or my parents could see me now . . . After barely a second I knock, which means I don't have time to think what the hell am I doing in this fucking corridor. I rush back into the room. He doesn't make me do it again.

He's still sitting on the bed and I position myself opposite it.

'Now stroke yourself for me. Stroke yourself as if you were discovering your body for the first time.'

Having understood the previous lesson, my hands come to rest on my body and work their way up towards my face. Without faltering, I run them over the back of my neck and slowly lift up my hair, closing my eyes as if trying to make him believe I really am enjoying what I'm doing.

I open them for a moment just to check how aroused Joe is and prepare myself for a potential onslaught of hands on me. I've got this all wrong. He's watching me the way he would a common porn film, with empty expressionless eyes. I carry on with my little performance, running my hands blandly over the tops of my breasts. I glance furtively at my watch which is still on my wrist. It's twenty-nine minutes past two. Only half an hour to go.

This all feels so unreal to me. I can't get into the character of the seductress – with or without the money. I'm too straightforward to pretend. I want to go home. What am I doing here? I can't bring myself to move my hands lower, they're stuck just above my groin. I'm not that good at acting.

'Touch yourself more, you've got to carry on arousing me.'

Obviously this isn't good enough for him. I'm completely lost again, feeling so hopeless I drop my arms by my sides. I don't know how to do this, where to put my hands. I feel clumsy and useless here in front of him but at the same time I feel I really couldn't care less any more. Two thirty-four.

'This isn't working. I can't do it.'

'I can see. You're more the type who likes to be dominated,' he says with an absurd teasing note in his voice.

I'm so nervous I feel like laughing at this pathetic attempt at flirtation, but I control myself. If you think about it, it's quite true: who wants to dominate someone if they feel no desire for them? Who even wants to participate? Well, only one sort of person: those who need money.

One simple answer, spoken in a childish voice, would have kept him happy: 'Oh yes, I want you to be my master.' Of course, I'm completely incapable of saying it. None of this is happening anything like I'd imagined it. I thought I'd be fucked quickly and that would be it. Just my luck to get a perv . . .

'Here, come and sit down on the bed,' he manages after twisting his lips in thought for a minute. 'I'll take matters into my own hands.'

He sounds firm, the serious bit's starting now. His fantasies are taking over.

I do as I'm told and find myself sitting beside him on the shabby bedspread which must have been here since the hotel first opened judging by its nondescript colour, struggling somewhere between blue and green.

Once again, I'm doing what he expects without batting an eyelid: one last effort, Laura. Two thirty-six. So I'm sitting on the bed with my breasts bare. His eyes, his whole face and his penis can't get enough of them. *Go on, have a good look, don't be shy.* If he goes on ogling them like this I might not even have to give him my whole body.

'Lie down on your back.'

Oops. He's not that stupid then. Two forty-one.

He puts his hand on the base of my neck and pushes gently downwards. I can feel his palm on my body for the first time, feel him touching me for the first time.

Lying on my back, I admire the flaking ceiling as I wait to feel his skin against mine. Just when I stop thinking about it his hand touches me, making me jump slightly, though I'm not really surprised. First, he starts with my stomach and moves up towards my neck. He probably means it to be sensual but it can't possibly have any effect on me. His other hand joins in too. The toing and froing on my upper body gets rougher, more intense, accelerating as his erection grows. I haven't opened my eyes once, trying to think of it all as a bad dream.

I can't work out whether feeling his old paws on me makes me want to be sick or to cry. I'm a dead body laid out on the bed. Well, he asked for a body and that's what he's got. If he asked me to do more right now I'd slap him.

Instead, the physical dance comes to a stop and he sits back up. I expect him to make some new bizarre request.

'Sit down, we're going to talk,' he says quickly.

I can't tell if this is a joke. Is talking to him in the contract? I imagine he can do whatever he likes – he is paying me.

'Why are you here today?'

The million-dollar question or how to get a student to own up.

'Have you got a boyfriend? What do you do in V?'

The questions are getting very personal. There's no danger of my giving him the real version of my life: it would be completely unbearable to give him even a hint of the life I lead. And, anyway, I'm not paid to tell the truth.

'No, I haven't got a boyfriend.'

Two forty-nine. Ten little minutes, but they could prove terrible.

'Is this money for you?'

I shake my head.

After pausing a moment, he says, 'What you're doing is a good thing.'

Really?

'I've got people who depend on me too, you know. I'm divorced and I've got a daughter. A bit older than you. I've remarried, a very beautiful woman, a while ago now. Sex with her isn't really happening. Anyway, I gave up on trying to share my fantasies with her long ago. You know, it's not easy having to face up to someone who doesn't want you any more.'

What's not easy for me at this precise moment is listening to his life story. I don't understand why he's decided to confide in me, when he's only just met me. If I go on listening to him I won't be able to help imagining his world, putting together images of who he is outside this hotel room. V isn't a huge place, and it would be perfectly possible to bump into Joe out for a family walk.

To think that when he leaves here he's bound to be going home to her. It sends a shiver right through me. I feel sorry for his wife and wonder what she would think if she knew her husband was regularly paying young girls and, on top of that, talking to them about her during his sessions.

'I don't want to know about your life.'

I'm fuming with irritation. Who does he think he is criticising other people when he hasn't got things exactly straight in his own head? I'm not saying anything more. I thought being a prostitute would just be a mechanical thing but here he is delving inside my head.

'Please tell me that with me you're combining a necessity with pleasure?' Joe says gently.

We've reached the pinnacle of absurdity now. I try to find something in his eyes or his tone of voice, some indication that he doesn't believe what he's just said for one moment. Not a bit of it. He really thinks I'm doing all this, not just for the money, but because – deep down – I actually like it. In his deranged mind, a woman can't give herself just for money, there has to be another reason. And, still in his deranged mind, I'm sure he enjoys thinking he's not as ugly as all that. Is it really that difficult for an old man whose own wife no longer wants him to acknowledge that my only motivation is financial?

So I don't say anything; I don't even feel angry any more, just a bit thrown. Then he goes back to his dance across my body with his hands, still touching my chest, breasts and stomach. The touch of his skin burns me, upsets me, but I don't let it show. He doesn't go lower down my body, my genitals are still virgin to his hands – a relief in the midst of my despair.

'Next time I'll bring you something. You'll like it, you'll see.'

Joe's already planning to see me again. Once again, I don't say anything, I can't exactly scream that that's out of the question.

'It's OK, you can get dressed again, it's time.'

Freedom, it's three o'clock! It's over. Very punctually, he gets up.

He rummages in his briefcase while I hastily get dressed.

'I'm really very pleased, you know,' he says, going back to his flattery. 'This first meeting's been fantastic. I've really enjoyed it. You're gorgeous, I wasn't expecting someone like you. And on top of that you're sensitive and pleasant, which I really like. All right, you had some reservations at the beginning, but I can be shy too. It'll go better in future, you'll see.'

He hands me an envelope and, right there in front of him, without even checking whether custom or good manners mean I should wait till I'm outside, I admire my booty. It's not a hundred euros that Joe's given me, as I was expecting, but two hundred and fifty! Two one-hundred euro notes and one fifty. I've never seen a one-hundred euro note before. My only concern about all this money is how I'm going to produce a one-hundred euro note from my pocket without arousing suspicion. I never spend that much; fives are more my usual fare.

'We'll see each other on the internet. But if you see me on MSN don't try talking to me, it's often my wife logging on in my name.'

With that we go down in the same lift that brought us up. The policemen are no longer at reception but, right now, I couldn't really care. I'm walking on air, my newly acquired money has given me wings. For now I'm in the clear, in one hour I've earned enough to deal with some bills that have been hounding me.

A whopping great 250 euros just to look at me – I really took him for a ride. What a mug, and to think he reckons we'll be seeing each other again. Never, it's over, once and just once. I'm worried he'll realise he's been had so I hurry off, just in case. I'm also keen to get away from that hotel and forget everything about it as soon as possible.

I'm feeling so relieved it's all over that I'm not really thinking about anything else. I haven't yet grasped that crafty old Joe manipulated me with his flattery and kind words, and knows exactly what he's doing.

All I can think about is this money which is now mine and will mean I can breathe for a while. I'll find a different solution next time. I pat my jeans pocket with its life-saving envelope and smile. Yup, just once, I smile in triumph.

Chapter 9

The Boyfriend

12 December 2006

I DON'T FEEL LIKE going straight to work after my meeting with Joe. I've got half an hour to spare so I call some friends and head for my favourite café, the one in the city centre run by my friend Paul.

When we meet up I smile normally. Nothing on my face betrays what I was doing half an hour ago. We joke about things – exactly what I need to stop me thinking about what's just happened. After a good hour checking up on all the latest gossip, the time's come to settle the bill.

'Look, girls, I'm really sorry, but I haven't got enough to pay for my coffee. Do you think you could pay for me? I'll pay you back soon, I promise.'

I honestly can't produce my one-hundred euro note here, or even the fifty. They wouldn't understand, given I never have any money. They know me well and know

I often can't pay my way. They pick up the till receipt without a word, splitting the bill between the two of them.

'No problem, Laura. It'll be your round next time,' one of them says, laughing.

She probably doesn't believe it. Most of the time I'm so skint I can't even pay for my own coffee. I often ask friends to come over to the apartment rather than meeting in a bistro, so that I don't have to beg. Still, when I get my wages, I invite them all out for a drink, just the one, but it evens things out financially.

Do they suspect something today? I'm trying my hardest to be me: happy and open. Things have been really tough recently but I've never admitted that to them. When they come to the apartment they ask whether I've got anything to eat and I joke about not having time to do the shopping.

Despite all the trouble I've gone to disguising my precarious situation, my friends are no fools. They may not gauge how bad it is, but can still see I'm struggling. They've been paying for my coffees for a long time now – they don't even notice any more. It still makes me feel awkward, though, but this time is worse, there's a heavy feeling inside me, laden with guilt. I've got the money in my pocket. I've got enough to pay for countless rounds with what I've just earned.

In the evening I meet Manu in a bar but don't order a drink for myself. I watch him finish his pint.

'How are you, gorgeous? What's your day been like?'
'Pff, just another day, nothing special.'

My arse! It's been anything but just another day but I can't exactly see myself confiding in him: 'Look, I'm fine, I've had a pretty normal day. Before work I let an old bugger I'd never met before fiddle with me. And the best bit is he paid me 250 euros. And all so I can give you money for the rent and bills while you smoke and offer everyone else drinks. Not bad, don't you think?'

When he seems satisfied with his blood-alcohol levels, we head back to our little 'love nest'. He makes me laugh on the way home, telling me silly stories. Manu's always more fun when he's got a few drinks inside him, in fact I think I prefer him like that.

We walk into the apartment in silence; the euphoria of the evening and of getting on well together is over. We get ready for bed like a couple who've been married twenty years. Given what he was like when we left the bar, I could try to turn him on a bit this evening. I do contemplate it, just for a minute.

Manu and I don't have sex very often: he can't always, as they say, rise to the occasion. I suppose it can happen to any couple that's together for a few years, and most like to think it will only be temporary. But it's beginning to feel like a long time to me and my DIY efforts are a bit boring. Unless he comes looking for it I gave up trying a while ago now. I've always been someone you could generously describe as 'eager', but I don't want him any more. I've been worried about this and have even spoken to my gynaecologist but she reassured me, saying this sort of thing often happens if you feel the other person no longer wants you. Bull's eye! What with his semi-erections and my vaginal dryness, we make a right pair. Like most people, I like sex and see it as an essential part of a relationship; so it's hardly surprising that ours is in such a bad way. I've got to the point where I just want him to fuck me. Before today. Because now I've realised I'll never want him again.

What's really odd is he doesn't seem particularly bothered about it. The only things he's been interested in these last few months seem to be going out with his friends and his course at uni. Although we haven't admitted it to ourselves, our relationship is in its death throes. We've accepted it, uncomplaining, because we know we can't actually do anything about it. When love disappears it's very difficult to rekindle it, even if you keep on and on trying.

So this evening, watching the pair of us brushing our teeth in silence in the bathroom mirror, I understand that this situation can't go on. Our relationship is a complete farce. Is it because of what happened this afternoon? That definitely had a catalytic effect, but the tension's been just below the surface for a while.

Is he going to talk to me, say anything at all? I feel deep inside me that, if he doesn't say anything, if he doesn't suspect what I've been through today, it will be hard for me to accept. It would mean he definitely doesn't know me the way he once did, because he used to know the minute something was wrong. I need his shoulders, and his arms to protect me and help me forget, just for this evening.

I slip between the sheets in bed. The silence weighs on

me so heavily. Not this evening, Manu, please, I beg you not to ignore me this evening, take me in your arms. He gets into bed beside me without even looking at me. He seems ready to get into what has become our usual sleeping position: with our backs to each other. I have to face full on the fact I've been refusing to see for months: our relationship's over.

Now that he's lying down and even after he's closed his eyes, I still hope he might start talking. I take the plunge: 'Goodnight.'

'Mm,' he answers sleepily.

Yup, goodnight, Manu. Goodbye.

Chapter 10

Loneliness

13 December 2006

THE SHRILL SOUND of the alarm clock wrenches me out of my deep sleep. I couldn't get to sleep last night, tossing and turning in bed as I went over what had happened during the day. I got up and smoked millions of cigarettes in the kitchen. I even tried to work on my Italian civilisation essay – unsuccessfully. My mind was too busy. It was only at about five o'clock in the morning, by which time I was really exhausted, that my eyes closed of their own accord.

Manu's still asleep. I gaze silently at his naked back turned away from me. I switch off the alarm and suddenly remember. Yesterday. The nightmare. The nightmares.

Since last night I know it's all over with Manu. Our relationship – which was a model of passion and friendship in the beginning – has gradually gone up in smoke and I haven't been able to do anything about it. I feel lonely getting up this morning, lonely facing my soul-destroying day. I'll always remember 12 December 2006 when my life changed so much.

But I've already run out of time to think. I need to get up and go to uni. There's only one thing I want: to bury myself in bed and cry. But that's not an option – I know that now. I'm going to have to carry on getting up every day. I'm going to have to live with the weight of that day on my shoulders. Right now I hate myself. Even in my pyjamas, hidden under all that fabric, I feel as if my body is tainted and exposed for all to see. I feel as if the horrible thing I've done is seeping from every pore, that no one can help noticing the ugliness radiating from me. I feel horribly dirty. Would it be even worse if Joe had had me completely?

I stumble to my feet. My body feels impossibly heavy. In the bathroom I let the water flow over me for quarter of an hour. At first I don't even move then I take a sponge and rub my skin as hard as I can. I inflict so much punishment on it that it starts going red. I couldn't give a stuff, I can't help myself. I want to get rid of all this crud and pretend yesterday never happened. I lost everything yesterday: Manu and my self-respect. For 250 euros.

I'm having to hurry now, not wanting to be late for the Métro. The real world is catching up with me so I don't even have time to feel sorry for myself because I need to get to uni. But how's this going to work? I know I won't be able to concentrate or listen or actually say anything. There are voices in my head which keep on and on telling me I'm just a prostitute. I've sold my body for money. I gave myself to a stranger for cash while my boyfriend was in lectures. I'm worthless and dirty, and it feels like I will be for the rest of my life.

I get dressed gently and quietly, and close the door of the apartment on my relationship with Manu. I'll never have that innocence in me now when I look at him. I haven't just cheated on him, it goes beyond that. I've cheated on myself, prostituted myself. The word rasps in my throat as I say it. But it just keeps coming back because that really is what happened.

There's a frost this morning. I walk quickly to avoid the icy wind and, maybe, because the speed might deaden my whirring thoughts. I feel a failure, ashamed, I haven't even got the strength to cry.

The journey to uni doesn't help much. When you sit down in the Métro you start thinking, going over things in your mind. Even if you don't want to, you have to think – about yourself, about life, about what you are. I sit there thinking, without even realising it, without meaning to. I feel as if everyone can tell what I did yesterday just by looking at me. I can feel myself blushing and bury my face in the big scarf round my neck.

Even if I stay with Manu I'm sure he'd work out what I've done sooner or later. My sin weighs too heavily on my mind for it not to show on the outside. I'm tired from my short night but I know I won't even be able to snooze today. All that hard work wasn't enough, I'm now going to have to pay for my mistake for the rest of my life with this constant thinking.

I come out of the Métro with my head in a whirl, my life's in a far worse state than before. There's one thing I'm sure of: my studies can be my refuge. Apart from them, Manu was the only thing worth putting my energy into, worth giving myself to. Now that that's all over I can't just let myself go. I've got to get a grip on my life again. I've done something wrong, but I've promised myself it will never happen again. And here's the proof: once was enough to make me lose the boy I loved. No, I'll never do it again.

Chapter 11

The Car Park

22 December 2006

'NEVER AGAIN!' Well, I should have expected this: now that I've paid the bills and given Manu the rent, I've got nothing left. The workhouse is beckoning again – I've got to find somewhere to sleep. But how? A friend at uni has agreed to take me in for a while. She lives alone in her apartment and I think, deep down, she's quite pleased to have some company.

I'm at hers then, getting ready to meet someone. I've answered one of those countless ads a second time: people asking for students are hardly in short supply so I had no trouble finding a new taker.

Life goes on with its day-to-day trials and I've gone along with it, trying to cope as best I can, but while I'm looking for a new apartment I inevitably come up against lots of expenses which I can't meet with the money from my telesales job. Once again, I've come to a dead end financially. It's no longer a question of just struggling. I feel that, if I don't do something, this will go on and on happening and I'll never keep my head above water. If I want to live in my own apartment this is the price I have to pay.

I've already got a job and my classes, what else can I do? I ask myself the question but I already know the answer. That door is still open in spite of all the promises I made myself.

I have mixed emotions about that first time with Joe – which, in my mind, wasn't really a first time because it was so far removed from what you would expect. Taking my clothes off in front of him and having to go along with his fantasies really shook me up but, even so, I still felt I'd taken him for a ride. It was a terrible first time, in fact, because now that I'm short of cash again I can't completely write off that option.

So I've got in touch with another man. Sitting in a trance in front of a secluded computer at uni, I gave in again. Still in the same state, I see this rendezvous just as a way of getting back on my feet and being done with all the expenses for the apartment. We've agreed on a rate of seventy euros an hour for two hours. Plus the restaurant which, obviously, he will pay for.

He's young, only twenty-six, and his name is Julien. Maybe it will be easier with him, I think to myself, than with someone old like Joe. I'm also curious about his motives, why he's prepared to pay a prostitute. I would have thought at his age it wouldn't be all that difficult finding a girl.

We've arranged to meet in a restaurant in the city centre. This time if I bump into someone it won't be much of a challenge finding an explanation. We're the same generation, which helps. People won't be tempted to speculate as they might have done if they'd seen me with Joe.

I don't have to wait for him, he's already there when I arrive. It only takes one look to understand why he contacted me – he's got frustration written all over him. Physically he's beyond ordinary: not particularly tall, or especially short and he carries himself with a sort of stoop. He's got terrible hair which, again, instantly pigeonholes him as boring. I think it's meant to be gelled and spiky but it all veers off to one side – no sense of style there.

His clothes leave a lot to be desired too, I think, starting to hate him. Limp wine-coloured woollen jumper, shapeless jeans and festering trainers. The general impression is slightly ridiculous. The sort of typical loser I'd never look at twice in the street. Unless, of course, he was as the butt of a joke between me and my girlfriends. Are we cruel? Maybe we are.

We've given each other a tentative peck on each cheek. He's clearly embarrassed and already seems to be regretting coming. As we go into the restaurant, I hope people don't think we're an item. Misplaced pride on my part. I'm glad I didn't get too dressed up for the evening: I'm just wearing jeans and a little top, quite sexy but not too much.

The place is just like him – nondescript. No form of decoration, white walls, tables in neat rows. The glaring white light is probably what bothers me most because it exposes us too much. Terrible, that's how I would describe the place. The owner hasn't even tried to give it a casual café atmosphere which I would have liked. I'm obviously dogged by bad taste in my experiences as a prostitute, so I'm constantly reminded exactly what I'm doing. Anyway, even if I liked this place, the fact that I'm here with a customer puts a mental block on ever coming back. A customer? Yes, a customer, because I'm on the game.

The waitress takes us to a table near another couple. The place is very full and the tables are all very close together. I can sense Julien tensing slightly; he would have preferred a more isolated position to avoid being noticed. Once we're settled we sit in silence for a moment, and I can tell he's rubbing his hands together nervously under the table, not sure how to get a conversation started. I think I'll help him a bit, not only out of pity but also because I refuse to spend the whole evening in silence.

'What do you do for a living?'

'I work for a company on the outskirts of V. It's quite interesting work and . . .'

It's only taken one sentence: I'm bored. I keep my eyes trained on him but don't listen to the rest, just letting my thoughts wander. Twenty-four hours later I won't have a clue what he's telling me this evening – I'll just remember a long tirade, a soporific monologue which he found reassuring and which meant he could disguise his obvious embarrassment. There's absolutely nothing interesting about this guy, just like his job.

Worried I might die of boredom and finding it difficult to go on hiding how effing tedious I'm finding this, I start stirring things up a bit. It's one of my biggest faults: the minute I see a weakness in someone, I'm cruel and make the most of it. I have plenty of doubts about myself, of course, but I never let them show, so I really don't understand people who can't cover theirs up. This guy's clearly a loser, I tell myself, and the really bad news for him is it comes across in everything he does.

I make no bones about butting into his mind-numbing drivel: 'Why are you here today?'

'Here? You mean why did I choose this restaurant?'

'No, come on! Here, with me. Why did you decide to put an ad on the net asking for a "masseuse"?'

He is visibly put out. The challenging, provocative note in my voice makes him uncomfortable. He's looking frantically left and right to see whether anyone's heard my question. I can already see the beads of sweat on his forehead. What a prat! Does he really think I'm going to spend the whole meal pretending I don't know he only wants to fuck me? Unless, deep down, he doesn't really know what he wants.

'Well . . . um . . . it's quite complicated, you know . . . I've never done this sort of thing before, this is the first time.'

Go on, spit it out, you can't get enough, can you? I'm getting really crude inside my head.

'Here goes: I'm married . . . to someone great, perfect in fact . . . but, well, when it comes to sex . . . I don't really know what's going on . . . it's complicated . . .'

'I'm sure it's not all that complicated. Your wife's frigid, is that it?'

You could say I'm not exactly mincing my words. He sits up in shock then lets his shoulders droop again, as if agreeing with what I've just said. This man's got taboos that I've walked all over in a matter of minutes. Stuff it, why should I be the only one to suffer?

'Um . . . yes, that's right. Let's say she doesn't really want me that way. At first, I thought it would sort itself out, it wouldn't last, do you see what I mean? We've been married a year now, but nothing's changed in terms of sex, quite the opposite. She rejects me the whole time and I daren't force her or talk to her about it. I don't have many friends I can talk to about it either and . . .'

It's now clear the poor bloke's in despair. Probably married too young to his childhood sweetheart, no mates to have a good time with, so he turns to prostitutes to drown his sorrows. He hasn't really got any social life and is trying to plug this gap with me this evening. He goes off into another endless soliloquy, telling me how lonely he feels, that he actually finds his work incredibly boring . . . and lots of other stuff I forget the minute he says it.

I interrupt him brutally once again: 'A relationship without sex is just friendship,' I say curtly.

He looks at me as if I've just said something terrible. I only half believe what I've said, but I find him exasperating and he makes me feel like being cruel. He looks crestfallen from my comment.

Right now I realise that being a prostitute doesn't stop at sex. Customers often contact professionals just to talk, to unburden their dull or thwarted lives. I'm not prepared to deal with this situation, listening to some rutting male whingeing. I've got my own problems and, even though I may not actually be suffering, it's already more than I can take. The conversation's taking a dangerous turn and heading towards something far too personal for my liking. I'm rapidly turning into his 'sex shrink'. This guy's forcing me to think and that shouldn't be compatible with the working-girl Laura. It's not the line of work I had in mind.

As the meal goes on I learn more and more about his life till I'm literally drowning in his day-to-day existence. The worst of it is, in any other circumstances, I'm sure I would have found him rather touching. In a different context I would probably have consoled him but, here, I just can't. I can't listen to his complaining any longer so I cut him dead: 'OK, say it, you need sex, don't you?'

He nearly jumps out of his skin. I'm scaring him, and I'm scaring myself. Being so crude and provocative. But I can't help myself. I'm fed up with this bloke beating about the bush so I'm taking things into my own hands to get the evening over with.

'Um . . . yes,' he eventually manages to whisper, relieved to be exorcised at last.

'Right, good. Well, we'd better get going then, don't you think?'

I can see he's panicking.

'Um . . . Go? Now?' he says.

'Yes, now. We've chatted enough for this evening.'

I can't take any more of this endless talking. The man got in touch with me for a 'massage' and instead we meet in this crumby restaurant and talk about his empty life. I want to bring this masquerade to an end as soon as possible.

'But where? In a hotel?'

'Have you got enough money for a hotel?'

'I don't know . . . you know . . . I don't know if I really want to any more.'

'Of course you want to. You got in touch with me so you must want to.'

He looks right into my eyes with that hangdog expression for several seconds. I've damaged his ego and, however low he may have already fallen, he's finding it hard to accept. I certainly won't contemplate going home without my money after an evening like this.

After a few minutes he says, 'I know a car park not far from here,' letting the words out with a sigh as if hoping not to need to say them again.

In a flash he pays the bill, gets me into his car and, without a word, drives to the aforementioned supermarket car park. It's a very dark night and it's hard to make anything out at all. It makes me feel protected; no one will see us.

Despite all the self-assurance he mustered when we left the restaurant, I can tell Julien feels very uncomfortable again when the time comes to cut the engine. He's rubbing his hands together nervously again and trying to create a diversion by fiddling with various knobs in the car. He's worried someone will find us here and I have to admit I feel the same.

'Are you cold?' he asks me.

It's the middle of winter and it is true that the chill of the night is beginning to catch up with us. It's a grim situation: the two of us, in a car in this car park, checking no one will see us fucking.

'Yes, a bit.'

'OK, I'll put some heating on.'

I light a cigarette without asking whether he minds. He turns up the heating and goes on rubbing his hands together as the warmth spreads through the car. Confronted with his indecisiveness, I decide to launch myself. I put my hand on his jeans, by his crotch. He hasn't got an erection. I look up at his face, trying to find an explanation . . . which I already know.

'I'm um . . . quite stressed,' he says, still looking just as miserable.

To stop him rambling on again I start rubbing his jeans more firmly. Without any response. I carry on with my task for a good five minutes, still convinced that if he doesn't get what he wants he'll bring the whole thing to an end and not pay me. After the psychological ordeal of this evening, I can't leave without some compensation.

Embarrassed not to be responding at all physically, he mumbles shyly, 'Maybe if you took all your clothes off . . .'

First initiative! I'm surprised by this unexpected comment: it's completely at odds with his tone of voice and behaviour. All the same, I take off my clothes, here in this car, lost in the middle of the car park. Right now there's only one thing I'm worried about: someone finding us. Julien obviously feels exactly the same.

After looking at my naked body for a few minutes he allows himself to touch it. I put my hand back on his jeans, in vain. First he touches my breasts and kneads them thoroughly. He clearly doesn't dare go further down and feels safer concentrating on my torso. He doesn't seem to be reacting to my hand rubbing his trousers. After a few minutes, desperate that the situation's drawing such a blank, he says, 'Hey, would you mind . . .'

I immediately understand what he wants. No need for a degree in prostitution for that.

I unbutton his trousers and start to perform fellatio. I feel him gradually becoming aroused. In no time, he's whipped off his jeans and lowered the passenger seat right down. He lies on top of me, puts on a condom and seconds later he's inside me.

I can't explain how I feel at the moment. Sickened, yes. My head's somewhere else, I can't feel anything any more. Julien has become 'him', an impersonal 'him'. The first 'him'. It's too much. I can't bear him inside me, I don't want him in me. Everything goes hazy and I close my eyes. I feel so dirty already. I clench my teeth with disgust. I feel terribly empty and the same words keep going round inside my head: now you really are a prostitute, abandoning yourself completely to a stranger's dick.

I don't look so clever now. No more provocation or

showing off. Actually, he's won in the end; he's the one who's getting what he wanted. I must think about the money, not forget what this is for, but it all feels too raw. I feel dispossessed of my own self. I've never felt so far removed from myself. I haven't any tears left to cry, just dizzy spells as proof of how tough my life is and bills piling up, forcing me to understand why I'm doing this. Where are you, Manu? How did I come to this? I don't want him to touch me any more, why do I have to put up with this? The situation feels so unfair I have to grit my teeth to stop myself crying out. *It'll be over soon, Laura, don't open your eyes, it'll soon be finished.*

I have to say he doesn't waste any time. He's come and now his conscience has taken over from his libido.

'Um . . . Laura . . . we'd better get going,' he says.

I don't look at him. I'm almost crying with joy to think it won't go on any longer.

'I'll pay you your two hours, don't worry. I'll give you the 140 euros.'

'Yes, OK.'

The money smells the same as the cash Joe gave me; the handing over process is hasty, taboo. Not at all easy.

'I'll drive you home, OK?'

I nod my head and we set off in silence. I can't utter a single word.

Long before we get to my friend's apartment, I ask him to pull over. We give each other a quick peck on the cheek, slightly embarrassed.

'Goodbye.'

'Goodbye, Laura. *Bon courage.*'

I get out of the car without a murmur and he drives off straight away.

Yes, courage, that's what I'm going to need. So that I accept not only the dirtiness but also the fact I'm already addicted to this money tumbling into my hand.

I hurry home through the freezing dark night. As Julien heads home to his wife waiting for him in their nice warm home, I go to sleep alone in my bed. I'm cold.

Chapter 12

Appearances

24 December 2006

MY MOTHER HAS LAID the table specially for the occasion with a multitude of different dishes, each one more appetising than the last. And I'm hungry as a wolf – which has become my default setting in the last three months. There are five of us for supper this evening: my father's invited a friend of his who would otherwise be spending Christmas alone. It always touches me when my father does things like this, but I don't understand why he doesn't extend the same kindness to me.

Having this friend here brightens the whole evening, and everyone's chatting happily. Everyone except me. I don't seem to be in party mood, I can't do it. These so-called Christmas holidays are more of a curse than a blessing for me. We've got exams right at the beginning of next term so I've got to revise more than ever. I'm still working for pitiful pay at the telesales company during the two-week break – I can't afford to take days off. I need to be earning money. But on the days I'm not working I don't know what to do with myself at home. Not going to lectures the last few days has really unsettled me. My studies are my refuge, the time when I don't have to think. Going to uni means getting away from home and having only a minimal social life. I've hardly seen my friends since September – my time is divided between uni and telesales. The rest of my spare time is completely devoted to studying, reading and revising.

This family reunion is a charade. My father's playing the perfect host, ostentatiously giving his friend a second helping. He's even all sweetness and light with me – he wants to look like the perfect, caring father. I listen to him talking, which he never does when it's just the four of us. He's a magician; he can transform himself in public and wear a mask.

It doesn't wash with me. Another year I might have accepted his little performance, even knowing he wouldn't speak to me the next day. I would have agreed to the pretence that we're very close just because it's what I absolutely long for. But it's different this year. I've had enough of begging for his love, I can't bear being ignored like this any longer. If he really were attentive he would have realised long ago that I'm struggling so badly: I've lost over two stone since September, I'm working myself to death and I'm reduced to tears every day. Maybe if he took the time to look closely at me he'd understand what I have to do for money.

I'm doing too much thinking to enjoy this evening. I'm ruining my father's plans – his guest can tell I don't feel like partying. I'm not bothered by my father's disapproving looks, I've had enough of playing a part. My mother does her best to fill the silent pauses. She's bound to be worrying that I'll make some insolent or nasty remark. My father's relying on my sister for conversation, asking her an avalanche of questions about school and her friends, bombarding her so she almost doesn't have time to draw breath. But she's delighted with the situation, feeling as if she's really being listened to for once.

After an unbelievably copious supper, it's now time to open our presents. My mother loves Christmas and makes a point of respecting tradition. She's put a large Christmas tree in the living room and arranged the presents beneath it. And, like every year, she's also got the whole crib out. No one in the family is a believer, not even her, but she loves going along with the whole thing. I know that in her heart of hearts she regrets not being able to give us a wonderful Christmas with loads of presents. So, almost as if she's compensating, she pushes the boat out with the decorations. I adore my mother and it really touches me how much trouble she goes to to make sure we're both happy, not just at Christmas, but all year round. She's a full-time broody hen, even though she's always talked to us as she would an adult. And her hard work pays off: seeing the sparkling tree and the crib with its little figures makes me happy to be here with her this evening.

No mountains of presents for us at Christmas – we're used to getting just one. Mum always manages to find us something that's particularly significant so that we forget that it is just the one. My sister and I don't really put much store by it all any more, but when we were little we would die with envy when our school friends showed off presents which looked like they were straight out of *The Thousand and One Nights*. Looking back, I can see it was a normal reaction.

This year, more than any other, I'm not expecting anything special. I haven't asked for one particular thing because I've got such an overwhelming feeling that I need everything. But 'everything' is out of reach for my parents; it would be utopia.

So here I am opening the present labelled for me. I slowly tear off the apple-green paper and find a pair of high-heeled black shoes. I saw them in a shop with my mum during the *Toussaint* bank holiday and I told her I liked them. I would never have thought she'd go back and buy them later. Even though I know he's had nothing to do with choosing my present, I thank my father from where I'm sitting. We don't kiss or hug.

I keep thinking about Manu. I haven't heard from him since we split up. My parents were relieved to hear we'd stopped living together; they've never really liked him and think he's a snob. I think that, in my mother's eyes, no one will ever be good enough for my sister and me.

If she only knew . . . She would definitely loathe Manu all the more. But first she would cry for days on end, then her sadness would turn to anger and she would try to find a culprit. At first she would blame herself, then Manu. If she found out everything he had made me pay for while he was spending virtually none of his own money, she would undoubtedly hold him responsible for my prostitution. She would go absolutely wild with rage, trying to find answers where there are none to be found. Over time, the whole thing would just become a bad memory and she would help me forget it, but she would spend the rest of her life licking that wound, holding it against herself for ever. No, she must never know.

The evening goes on quite peacefully, with no raised voices or arguments. I decide to go up to my room fairly early: I need to be up in good time tomorrow to revise. In the afternoon I'll catch the train back to V because I'm working for the telesales company from the twenty-sixth. No downtime really, but it'll pay off in the end, it just has to.

I hurry off to bed, giving everyone a little wave. Up in my room I start looking at one of my Spanish texts. I can't help it: the minute I have some spare time, I revise. I know I won't have any trouble passing my exams, I've worked hard for them, but I can't help myself, I'm a perfectionist, everything always has to be perfect. And, anyway, working stops me thinking about other things.

The very next day I'm on a train taking me back to V and, as usual, there isn't much to tell anyone about the two days spent with my parents.

Chapter 13

Oppression

7 January 2007

UNFORTUNATELY, MY EXPERIENCE with Julien hasn't stopped me. It's had exactly the opposite effect. There are always more new ads on the internet and I sometimes feel the world is full of frustrated people who'll never be satisfied. Mind you, I'm not sneering at them, given that these strangers and their rampaging urges are helping me out temporarily with my financial problems.

So I make contact with an older man, almost certainly for fear of landing another indecisive penniless bloke like Julien. This time his name's Pierre. The only thing I know about him is what he does: he's a businessman in a well-known company. I find that reassuring because it suggests a really solid financial basis. Making the decision in the first place is hard enough and this world really is like Russian roulette so I might as well make sure – as far as I possibly can – that I'll be paid. We've arranged to meet in the early afternoon on the large square in the centre of the city. He'd rather meet in the city centre and then go back to his place where, he makes a point of saying, 'we won't be disturbed'. At first I objected: there was no question of my going to some complete stranger's place, where all sorts of things could happen to me. But after some thought, he managed to persuade me: there would be no danger of being seen by anyone because his place was empty. He's keen on his anonymity, too, and doesn't want to run the risk of meeting in one of the city's hotels where he could bump into people. So our last email agreed that he would come and pick me up discreetly in his car, then drive me back to his place. I like to think I'll know whether I can trust him when I see him. I've gauged the dangers I'm exposing myself to by doing this, but I need the money. I want more and more now.

At the appointed hour, I head for the famous square in the city centre. I'm wearing one of my favourite dresses: grey with puffy tops to the sleeves, it shows off my waist and reveals a bit of leg, above my über fashionable boots. I feel very elegant in this outfit and I know it has an effect on men. It gives me a girl-woman appeal that turns heads. I've put it on with clear financial aims: the better I look, the more he'll be prepared to pay. And it's a beautiful, sunny winter's day: I got up early and just felt like looking pretty. For myself, not for him. As I walk, I can already see men staring at me and silently admiring my dress. Yup, I know I look good today.

In the distance I can see bustling stalls with people crowding round the produce on display. I forgot! There's a farmers' market today where inquisitive tourists come and buy things from local smallholders. That's good and bad: with so many people around, I can easily disappear into the crowd, but at the same time I could come across someone I know, and that thought soon becomes an all-consuming fear.

I decide to wait a little way back from all the activity so that I can quickly spot this Pierre and take him further away. He said he would be wearing a dark suit and a red scarf, something easy to spot but justified by the cold weather.

I scan passers-by and am already running out of patience after five minutes. I feel very uneasy and can't stop patting my hands against my crossed arms. I'm convinced people around me have noticed how strangely I'm behaving, which makes me even more paranoid.

All of a sudden I hear someone calling my name behind me, someone with a more than familiar voice. I recognise it instantly and it makes my blood run cold.

'Laura! Laura!'

I admit I'm tempted not to turn round, to run away like a coward. Instead I turn my head slowly, wanting to appear natural.

'Mum? What are you doing here?' I'm stuttering, trying to control the panic inside.

My mother. Here on the main square. While I'm waiting for a customer who's going to pay me to give him my body. I've turned to stone, like a child caught with her fingers in the jam before tea time. I stammer at her, knowing that if I can't speak intelligibly my mother will be suspicious, she'll know something's not right.

'You knew all the family were coming down from Nantes to see us today, didn't you? Do you remember? We thought it would be nice to spend some time in V together, to show them the city.'

Yes, utterly charming, right. Behind her I spot my father and the aforementioned representatives of what she calls 'the family'. I'd completely forgotten these factors: the farmers' market, my relations here for the weekend and my parents being perfectly capable of coming to the effing market. What a pretty picture: my mother, my father, my uncle and aunt and a couple of other strangers I've only seen two or three times in my life but who I recognise as part of my family tree. I'm cornered. I need to come up with something right away. I try not to look around for this unknown Pierre but I can't help the occasional furtive glance left and right.

My mother must know I'm not really listening to her but she can't possibly guess why. Enthused by this unexpected coincidence, she turns to the family members behind her to announce the happy news. I'm worried some big man in a red scarf is going to turn round and start talking to me if they say my name too loudly.

'Hey, look who's here! It's Laura!'

'Oh, you don't say, it's Laura! What a lovely surprise! You've changed so much. Quite the young lady. Were you coming to join us?' my aunt says ecstatically.

I like my aunt a lot, even though I don't see her very often, but I really couldn't give a stuff about her today. Through no fault of my own, I've ended up bang in the middle of a major family reunion in a public square while I, the prostitute, am waiting for a customer. And, anyway, what an idea to arrange to meet here in the middle of the afternoon! I was so stupid, but it's too late to moan about it now, I need to get out of this situation as quickly as possible.

Then I suddenly spot a red scarf wafting on the wind in the crowds. The man wearing it has his back to me and is walking towards the middle of the square. He must have been waiting on the sidelines too and, having not yet seen me, must be having a good look round to make sure he hasn't been tricked. About fifty, wearing a suit like he said, and very elegantly turned out. I know straight away this is my man.

My aunt, still waiting for an answer, snaps me out of my dazed state. 'Hello-o, Laura! Wake up!'

She and my mother turn round to see what the hell I'm staring at so intently. Luckily for me, Pierre the business-man has disappeared into the crowd.

'Um . . . Sorry, I was miles away,' I say with a smile to stop them looking any further. 'I've been waiting for some friends for a quite a while and I thought I'd seen them but it wasn't them.'

I hastily grab my mother and my aunt by the arm and take them in the opposite direction to where the man is. As if we were three good friends. My father and the rest of the family start following us, chatting all the way.

'Of course, the girl's busy. Well, what do you expect at her age? We won't keep you any longer, lovely Laura. We'll get back to our shopping. You know this is such a beautiful place!'

She can't stop talking – my aunt's such a chatterbox. And my ageing businessman must have left. The thought of losing money because I've bumped into my family is overwhelming. Even though these two worlds that should never meet have come so close today . . . I still need the money to keep my head above water. I know I'm playing with fire, but a voice inside me keeps telling me there's nothing else I can do.

I can't help myself, my eyes are frantically scanning backwards and forwards again. My aunt doesn't seem to notice but my mother can see how impatient I am.

'Come on, we'll carry on now. You have a nice time with your friends, sweetheart. Come and have supper at home this evening if you like. We could drive over and pick you up after our shopping, you can spend the night at home and catch the train back in the morning. I know it's a bit of a journey but . . . Unless you've got plans already . . .'

'I'll see, Mum, thanks for asking. I'm not sure what I'm doing yet. I've got work tomorrow, you know.'

I'm actually working at the moment. The goodbyes to my family seem to go on for ever. My aunt gives me a long hug and whispers that she hopes she'll see me this evening, that I'm so pretty, that blah blah blah . . . My father, on the other hand, gives me a little wave without really looking at me. Can he somehow see the sin written on my face?

I skip off, looking nonchalant but my head's whirring. I try to be discreet as I look around to find my man – I know my mother's still watching me. I cross my fingers that he hasn't done a runner because I'm so horribly late.

As I search for a scarf, I suddenly spot it at the far end of the square. I've done such a good job of getting my family away from him that he's now right over at the other end so I'll have to be discreet again. I'm determined to have this money today. Bumping into my parents was a wake-up call but I haven't got time to think about that or worry about it.

I eventually reach my businessman and slow down to avoid attracting attention. He doesn't know who to expect because I didn't describe myself and, right now, I'm glad I didn't. He's pacing up and down in front of me, so I fall in step behind him then slip past him. As we draw level, I sound like a professional dealer as I mutter: 'I'm Laura, follow me, don't turn round and just keep walking, my family are here.'

The whole sentence comes out in one quick breath. I can feel the pressure around me. I want to get away from this oppressive situation as soon as I can.

I can feel him walking behind me, carefully following my every step. I keep up my furiously athletic pace for a good five minutes without turning round once. When I'm finally convinced that we're no longer in danger, I stop in a deserted street to catch my breath.

I turn to face him: he's quite tall and not that bad for his type. Standing there in his suit you can tell he's going for a sort of James Bond look. Pretty successfully in terms of classiness, not so much for his speedy reactions. Now that I can see his figure close up, I'd say he was over fifty. Still, it's definitely shown off to best advantage in that suit. But the minute I look up at his face I'm disappointed. His eyes are a pale blue which, in itself, is quite captivating, but they're completely devoid of spark. He looks as if he's been through ten years of toil and exhaustion, and hasn't got anything left to give.

What with him dressed up as an elegant businessman and me done up as a sexy young student, we make a right pair: a father with the daughter he brought up well and taught to dress nicely ... but definitely not an eighteen-year-old prostitute and her client.

'Hello, Laura. That was quite a pace!'

He speaks so slowly that I've already forgotten the beginning of his sentence – even though it was so short!

'Hello, Pierre. It is Pierre, isn't it?'

'Yes, it is. What do you say to going and sitting in a bar for a bit to recover? Then we can set off.'

There's a swanky bar on the corner of the street which provides us with a refuge. Firstly, because neither of us wants to carry on running through the streets, but also because I'm keen to hide myself away as soon as possible. I've been too visible already today. We choose a table at the back.

Once we've ordered our drinks we sit in silence for several minutes, which gives me a chance to have a look at the place. The waiters are well suited to the setting: good-looking and very cool. Mind you, they're giving us funny looks and whispering amongst themselves. At first it annoys me that the one who brings our drinks doesn't acknowledge my 'thank you' or the smile I give him. Then, in a flash, I realise why he's so cold: the boy can tell we're not father and daughter, despite our crafty disguises. I can picture him talking about me to the others behind the bar while he makes coffees for more reputable customers: 'Oh, come on, I swear that one's a pro. And he's either her pimp or her next trick. It's so obvious.'

Is it really all that obvious? Pierre doesn't seem to have noticed anything and I daren't mention it to him.

'Let's finish our coffees, then shall I take you to my place?' he asks easily.

Yes, the sooner the better. Halfway through a gulp of coffee I nod my head in agreement. One thing I can tell for sure after spending only a few minutes with him is that he hasn't got the oomph to do me any harm. But I'm still on my guard; I have to be careful because still waters run deep, as they say.

'It'll be more private than a hotel, there's no one at home at the moment. I'm sure you're going to like it, it's beautiful. I'm lucky I actually own . . .'

After Julien, there's no way I'm going through all that again. I don't want to know anything about his life and I tell him so straight away. That's the sort of thing that makes me hate going into cafés with customers: it encourages a palliness I can't deal with. I wouldn't make a good escort girl.

Five minutes later we're outside walking towards his car. While he acts like a Formula One driver at the wheel of his luxury car, I daydream about where he's taking me: a lovely big house with a large garden, far on the outskirts of the city with no near neighbours. One day, I'll have a place like that myself.

Pierre doesn't say anything, which gives me more time than I need to panic and start gauging the consequences of what I'm doing. At the end of the day, I've no idea where I'm going or what I'll find there. I've taken risks this time. Who knows, this gentlemanly suit who speaks more slowly than his own shadow might turn out to be a coke addict in need of a fix and once he's had it he might pounce on me. Mind you, judging by what he's like now (taking a good ten minutes to check the coast is clear before pulling out at a T-junction), I doubt it.

When he stops after only a fifteen-minute journey, we're opposite some huge luxurious apartment blocks in a smart part of town. They're very modern, just on the edge of the town centre. The view from the top must be magnificent. Pierre gets out of the car, his slow footsteps making him seem older in spite of his dynamic business suit. The walk to his apartment is as long as it's agonising.

We get to his floor at last. The lavish corridors are clean cut, empty, spotless. Everything rich people like. We could easily be in a massive private home. Now we're outside his door and I realise we've got the whole ordeal of the key to get through. I feel like snatching it out of his hand and turning it in the lock myself. I'm fed up with him already and I can tell that time's going to pass very slowly while I'm with him.

Luckily, I'm momentarily distracted from this dismal thought when we finally get into the hall. Pierre the snail crawls in the vertical position towards the kitchen, leaving me to admire his apartment for a moment. The first room I can see is the living room: it's fantastically big and all in white, like a perfect cliché from a rapper's video. The sunshine really shows off his top-of-the-range furniture – the whole effect is minimalist and the few ornaments dotted about on shelves are African statuettes in ebony. Pretty good taste, I would say, and on a huge scale.

I'm torn between an inevitable feeling of modesty in the face of so much opulence and a strange kind of pride tinged with a hint of relief: he didn't lie, he makes a lot of money. All that matters right now is that I haven't ended up in an ambush surrounded by a gang of his debauched, lusting friends.

I don't have time to congratulate myself for my good luck – well, relatively speaking – before the sluglike Pierre appears with some things on a tray. He puts it down on the coffee table in the living room, then turns to me and says, 'There, I thought you might like a little something before . . .'

His unfinished sentence is left dangling. We both know how it ends. I have a look at the food on offer. He's brought me a glass of milk and a slice of gingerbread. Shit! He really thinks I'm a little girl. He's playing out the fantasy of the child-woman to the bitter end. I haven't really thought about the image I give off to customers. Or is it just him? Because of my girlish dress?

So Pierre thinks of me as child, one he'd be more than happy to fondle. Something's wrong with this picture. I accept the snack without a word, quickly picking up the cake to soothe my hunger and drinking the glass of milk.

Pierre is standing with one hand on his hip in a position that looks completely unnatural. He watches me nibbling at the cake and smiles, proud of his child feeding herself to keep her strength up. I quickly drop the piece of cake when I see his expression.

I'm about to light a cigarette when he says, 'Ah, but you can't smoke in my apartment.'

My only reaction is to look him dead in the eye as I exhale the smoke. This upsets him and he doesn't know how to respond so he turns his attention to something else.

'Some music?' he says suddenly.

Armed with the remote control, he tries to start the music centre, which doesn't seem to want to obey him. For a minute he carries on irritably trying to get it to work before going and seeing what the problem is for himself. The height of absurdity: a rich businessman who buys things for the simple reason that they're expensive, but doesn't know how to use them. His attempts to create a sensuous atmosphere are pathetic. Everything he's been planning so minutely is falling flat. I've even stopped smiling, the man's so boring.

After several minutes of fussing, the music finally puts in an appearance. I recognise it straight away – Luz Casal. A singer with a celestial voice that's lulled me through my childhood and teens. She's my father's favourite singer. She's literally part of the family: we know all her albums, not just the ones that have made her famous recently. I've never wondered whether or not I like her music: her CDs are constantly playing at home. I was introduced to her at a time when you don't question your parents' taste: you like what they like because you love them. That's why Luz Casal naturally comes to mind when I think of home and my family.

Pierre couldn't have made a worse choice. I've had a very unusual relationship with this woman, an untouchable relationship that he mustn't be allowed to taint. Sitting cross-legged by the coffee table with my mouth full of gingerbread, I think it's outrageous that he can disturb the harmonious connection between Luz Casal and my family. Once again – and once too many times, I would say – my private life has become dangerously mixed up with my life as a prostitute. I know deep down that Pierre hasn't done it on purpose and, because he doesn't know me at all, he couldn't have guessed. But I still can't help hating him, right now, just for making me think.

My eyes must really be like daggers because he's been staring at me for a while trying to interpret my thoughts.

'I hate this woman,' I say sharply. 'Could you switch it off please?'

Surprised that I've suddenly broken my silence, Pierre obeys what sounds more like an order than a request for a favour. The room falls silent again.

Almost certainly to avoid conversation, he comes over to me – slowly, of course. As he gets closer I can tell he is getting aroused. The room stinks of sex with every step he takes. I don't move; I can't make up my mind to touch him of my own free will.

I watch him make his way over to me. When he reaches me, his crotch is literally on a level with my eyes. He stays like that for several seconds, obviously enjoying it. He unbuttons his suit trousers and slips them down his legs. The whole situation makes me feel sick. I know I've reached my limit today. I promise myself I won't give him anything. It's too late for him: right now I stupidly hold him responsible for my sad circumstances and my prostitution. So far this rendezvous hasn't gone at all as it should have. He's got everything wrong. Even the way he blinks is so lazy I find it exasperating.

Confronted with my passive response, he eventually reaches out his hand to lift me to my feet. Standing next to him, I realise how tall he is: the top of my head comes up to his mouth.

Pierre takes off my dress. I'm now standing in front of him in my underwear, my legs slithered into cheap stockings. It doesn't matter much to him, he likes what he sees; I can tell from his panting breath. He leads me to his room and pushes me gently down onto his enormous bed. While I'm lying down he takes off his shirt then leans towards me and, with one simple move, turns me over onto my stomach. I let him manhandle me like a blow-up doll.

'I'm going to give you a massage. Would you like that?'

'Mm . . . yes, yes . . .'

Pierre lies full length on top of me. I'm crushed beneath his weight. I free myself by bucking my hips upwards, startling him. Once free, I can breathe normally again. Then he lies alongside me and starts fondling me. He's left my bra on and I suspect that's because he doesn't know how to undo it. I feel like running away. I'm beginning to struggle with a new dilemma: maybe I should just leave after all, if this doesn't feel right. A glance at his clock radio tells me there's barely twenty minutes to go. The lure of the money helps me make up my mind. I'm prepared to wait, for the sake of this cash which I feel I've more than earned.

His hands are wandering over my body at the anticipated rate, no surprises there, too slowly to help pass the time. I'm completely motionless: if anyone came in now they might think I was dead.

For exactly eighteen minutes he rubs himself up against me without trying anything else. My stony silence must be too off-putting for him to venture further. He doesn't say anything, making do with this physical contact. I close my eyes; it's the best thing to do. When the red glow of his alarm clock finally announces that I'm saved, I jump out of bed without a word. Pierre gets up, docile to the last, not even sighing at my obvious haste to get away.

Still silently, I swivel my eyes at him to make him follow me to the living room. He puts his paternalistic hand into his wallet, like a daddy agreeing to give his little girl a few notes so she can go out and have fun with her friends. He takes out 150 euros, for two hours. Handsome dividends for what he took – hardly anything. All the same, I feel strongly that this money was hard earned and is well and truly owed to me.

Even though I've trusted him since I met him in the city centre, I know I'll never see Pierre again. He's too closely associated with a feeling of disgust. And, more particularly, with my parents' ill-timed appearance. Rationally, I know this could have happened to anyone but my mind is stubborn and can't help making the connection with him, holding him responsible. It's because of him that I went to the square today, because of him I had to lie to my family (although, for now, all I've done is 'fail to mention' something).

Pierre offers to drive me back but I decline: no chance of spending another minute with him. If it was two days' walk back to V I'd do it. I take the money, practically snatching it from his hands, and run for the door without another word. I leave Pierre on his own in his lavish castle. When I walk through the door I don't even turn round as I mutter an inaudible 'Goodbye.'

'We'll we be in touch soon then, Laura.'

'Um . . . Yes.'

I don't believe it for a minute. But I'd rather lie to avoid endless explanations and, more to the point, so he doesn't get annoyed with me. I know my lie is safe; the man's only got my email address, nothing else.

When I get outside the building, in the fresh air, I stop and look up at the sky. That's it now, I'm completely cornered. I'm going to have to lie to my parents when

they ask me how I've spent my day, and turn down their
invitation to supper to avoid accusing looks from my
father – the one person who knows so much, who may
have guessed everything.

I really feel I've prostituted myself now. On the game,
that's what I am. Because I know I'll do it again; and that
the Juliens, Joes and Pierres can't do anything to change
that. I've become a prostitute because I've started
banking on the money from my tricks to make ends
meet. I'm the whore who, for a couple of hours, can
forget the hands fingering her body. A part-time low life,
a student tart, a computer hustler. In the outside air I get
some colour back in my cheeks. Gently, with my heart
pounding in my chest, I head over to the nearest bus
stop.

Chapter 14

Nerves

14 January 2007

TRUDGING THROUGH THE COLD with my coat buttoned up to my chin, I have to run to make sure I'm on time for my first university exam. I'm stressed about today because it's a literature exam. Of course I've read all the books, but only at the last minute. I couldn't buy the things, given how prohibitively expensive they are, and had to wait till I could get them through the university library ... which only happened last week, and I had to gobble down three books on the trot. I'd already learned the work on them which was stupid because, without knowing the books themselves, it obviously meant nothing. So last week was full of adrenaline. I kept dashing from work to revising to catching the Métro for uni, with the stress of exams on top.

Now that the time has come for the first test I'm really worried. I run through the corridors to get to the building where they're holding the exam. When I arrive there's already a little gathering outside the amphitheatre. When you've been running from the moment you get up and then finally stop moving, you suddenly realise just how tired you are. The only thing keeping me on my feet is nervous energy.

I saw a customer two days ago. This time I decided to keep part of my earnings for a little treat; I'm going to do a bit of shopping. That's the problem with easy money. You always want more.

I went to see this man then. All he was looking for was someone to 'carry out household duties in her underwear'. With exams looming, I was just as desperate for money, but was so jittery I was even less inclined to let anyone touch me. So I spent two hours at this man's house, ironing his shirts in my bra and knickers, that's all. He slipped me 100 euros.

In the Métro on the way to uni this recent escapade came back to me and I suddenly felt dirtier than ever. I know mid-term exams aren't the best time for developing self-confidence, but I couldn't help loathing myself, telling myself I'd never get through them. Prostitution became a drug the minute my salary from the telesales job wasn't enough. When I thought about all the money I could make, I even contemplated giving up those phone calls and 'devoting' myself entirely to prostitution. No more crippling shift schedules, I could just work a few hours a month and earn three times as much.

But, however boring and badly paid it may be, that telesales job is the only thing – along with uni – which keeps me grounded in reality, in real life. If I only worked as a prostitute I think I'd very soon fall head first into a prostitution ring with a pimp in control. He'd make me give up uni and I'd become his goose laying golden eggs for him full time.

Outside the amphitheatre the pressure's mounting by the minute. I've got to calm down if I want to keep my head for this exam. I try to reassure myself: it's completely normal to feel like this, it's my first university exam and I love my course so much that it feels like there's a lot at stake. There are exams all through the week, I've got to cope with the pressure. The only test I'm not worried about is the oral because I've always found expressing myself easy. I've just got to get through the literature; once I've done that, I'll be more relaxed.

I rummage in my coat pocket for my tobacco. I've only got a few crumbs left. So, as usual, I ask my friend if she can let me have a cigarette. What a luxury, a real cigarette before an exam – it must be a good sign!

The doors to the amphitheatre open and I go in, determined to show what I'm capable of.

Chapter 15

A Meeting

24 January 2007

PAUL'S BAR SEEMS to have become my home territory of its own accord. I first found it a long time back, way before I became a student. I immediately felt comfortable in the place. The décor has a colonial feel to it with dark wood. There are lots of pictures of actresses from the 1940s on the walls and, even though I don't know who most of them are, they soon felt familiar. Still, I didn't go that often because I wanted it to create that same magical impression every time. Paul would nod hello when I dropped in from time to time and we'd exchange a few words. In the early days, I took refuge here after each 'professional' rendezvous. Then I started coming more and more regularly: before or after work, for a coffee or an impromptu chat if I bumped into some friends.

The radical change to how important it is in my life only happened when I scuttled back to safety here after my meeting with Joe. Ever since then I associate the bar with a feeling of relief, of comfort after physical and emotional upheaval. I can drown my sadness and darkest thoughts here, forgetting everything about my life. It's a halfway house between the seedy hotels and my apartment; I've really made a cocoon of the place.

Over time I've become friendly with Paul, the waiter. I like having him around. I talk to him quite openly, though I never go into details. Partly because I don't want to (I'm not the sort of girl who tells her life story to everyone she meets), but also because Paul's quite superficial. He wouldn't be in the least bit interested in what I had to tell him, except for the sex bits. I really can't stand it when you're talking to someone and they keep looking around for something more interesting to latch onto. Given how little I trust him as a 'lifelong keeper of innermost secrets', I've completely ruled out admitting anything to him about my forbidden activities. I still can't imagine revealing a secret like that to anyone. I don't want to have to justify myself, to see the look in his eye which might not go so far as to judge me but would definitely pity me. Come to think of it, I don't think he'd believe me anyway.

Paul is a skirt-chaser. He's got a huge ego and he flirts with every girl who comes into his bar. Super-quick conquests. He shags them and then dumps them a few days – even a few hours – later. In fact he tried his luck with me at first. I think he's set himself the task of seducing every pretty girl who steps through the door. He sweet-talked me quite a bit but there's no way I could be interested in him: he's too closely associated with my life as a prostitute. He could tell there was no point and soon struck me off the list of potential prey. I don't think he was really interested in me, he just saw me as another conquest, and he certainly wasn't prepared to put in any extra effort to achieve his ends with me rather than someone else. It's not really his style to go to any trouble over a girl. I also have to remind myself that, because he's geographically so close to the places where I have my mysterious meetings, he'll eventually work out where I'm going and what I'm doing – if he can be bothered.

At the height of my time as a prostitute, the bar will become a second home to me. I admit that the other customers have a lot to do with that. Most of them are in their thirties: crisp young businessmen or struggling artists, the odd model, the place never feels old or boring. All these people mingling happily at the bar, their voices blending into a harmonious hubbub.

I've always felt more mature than other girls my age, and as I chat to complete strangers – but these are strangers of about thirty – I realise I feel most comfortable with that age group. Ever since I was little I've had to grow up more quickly than others, and my parents brought me up with a strong sense of responsibility. So I had real problems with all the childishness and pranks at school. Sometimes my friends were fun but most of the time I couldn't believe the sort of things they said. I couldn't stand them gushing, 'Oh, you'll never guess, my boyfriend's got a car!' My boyfriend at the time was thirty years old and had had a car for a while. So nothing exceptional about that, as far as I was concerned. I couldn't motivate myself to join in their plans for weekend sleepovers or their first experiments with so-called soft drugs.

As a general rule, I went to school for my lessons and left as soon as I could. I rarely mixed with other people there. It's not that I was haughty, I just didn't naturally mix in with them. I liked having them around during the course of the day but never really 'made friends' or arranged to meet them outside school. It was the same with boys. For as long as I can remember I've always found boys my own age incredibly boring, except for Manu who's more or less the same generation as me. When I was old enough to start going out with boys I never considered my peers as potential boyfriends. I prefer more accomplished men who aren't going through some post-adolescent crisis or trying to find their own identity. Sometimes I regret growing up so quickly because at school I felt lonely, misunderstood and out of step with what was going on and what I was experiencing. I think like a thirty-year-old; my mind is ten years ahead of my age. At the end of the day, I would like to have fun like a girl my own age, doing silly superficial things and not always thinking like a responsible adult. I sometimes feel tired of being who I am but I can't help myself: I've got to face the fact that I'll never be someone who likes childish fooling around, even just for a bit. I haven't been that naive for a long time.

That's one of the reasons I immediately felt at home in

Paul's bar. I almost always come here alone, knowing I'll end the evening chatting to someone new.

When I get to Paul's bar this evening the place is packed. There's a rock band playing and a gaggle of half-drunk customers have turned the bar area into a dance floor. Their good mood is infectious and I catch myself smiling the minute I step through the door. Paul sees me and quickly brings me a glass of wine, to 'relax me' he says. I know that he's actually showing off to the men leaning up at the bar who are having a good look at me while I kiss him hello. It's his way of saying, 'Yup, lads, I know her.'

Well, it works. Two of them try to strike up a conversation with me straight away.

'Hello, do you often come to this bar?' one of them begins, not very originally.

'I've never seen you here and I know I wouldn't have forgotten a pretty girl like you!' the other says, full of inspiration.

How imaginative! Their opening gambits are bargain basement material. I can sense a man's sexual intentions at a hundred paces. I answer their questions like a good girl and even allow myself to ask a few bland questions of my own, out of courtesy. The two blokes know each other well and, as we talk, the conversation gets competitive. Which of them will be taking the girl home this evening? Whoever formulates the sentence that coaxes the biggest smile out of me? I force myself to stay polite but I'm dying to walk off so that they grasp the fact that they haven't got a hope in hell with me.

All of a sudden I spot him behind the two men. He's been watching me for several minutes. Brown hair with a few stray locks hiding his eyes, which I think are probably green. He's wearing a striped cotton shirt with the sleeves rolled up. Very average clothes but, in spite of that, the moment I notice him I can't stop looking at him. He's captivating. There's something kind and friendly about the way he looks at me. It's not the first time I've seen him here. I've seen him chatting with Paul over a cup of coffee a few times. I smile as I contemplate serving him up the standard issue 'Do you come here often?'

He's trying to communicate something to me with his eyes but I don't have time to interpret it. Two seconds later he's next to me, putting his hand round my waist in front of the two flirting competitors. I hardly need say they straighten themselves up pretty sharply, ashamed to have got things so wrong. Silence descends on us, punctuated by their embarrassed coughs and throat clearing.

'Oh . . . Hi,' one of them manages to stammer.

A couple of polite niceties later and they've withdrawn. The saviour turns my body round to face him without letting go of my waist. The situation is terrifyingly erotic and I feel a shudder run through me, making the hairs on my arm stand on end. I can't take my eyes off him and he watches my face without a word. He's really not what you would call good-looking, but I'm fascinated by him. I could stay like this for an hour but after a minute or so, I decide to break the silence.

'Thanks, they were becoming quite a pain.'

'Yes, that's what I thought.'

He points to a table that's just been left empty, then orders us a couple of beers and, just like that, quite naturally, we spend the evening together, laughing a lot and talking about our day-to-day lives. His name is Olivier. He doesn't do much in life and even seems a bit bored. He looks and lives a bit like a Bohemian. Unless someone comes up with a time-machine, he seems resigned to the fact that he won't be able to go back to the 1970s. He got the wrong decade when he was born.

It's a happy, comfortable evening, I feel great. I don't know why everything suddenly seems so easy. And I don't try to work out why it is you sometimes feel so at home with a complete stranger, even down to telling him very personal things. I talk about my family, my course at uni and Manu. He listens attentively and tells me about the events and experiences that marked his child-hood and the more recent past. It's a healthy balanced exchange, each of us giving a little of ourselves. And it's all done with smiles; even pain and suffering come across as constructive trials.

The drinks keep coming as the night wears on. We're getting more and more drunk, launching us into the peculiar logic of alcohol which makes us reveal every-thing about our lives quite readily and without any hang-ups. I've got this strange feeling I can tell him everything, even and particularly the one thing I'm hiding from everyone else. More than once I catch myself wondering how he would react if I told him about my debauched activities. He's the one who makes the first move towards major confessions.

'You see, after thirty years, I feel as if nothing can shock me now. Don't you think that's a shame?'

The opportunity's too irresistible and my secret's too heavy for me to go on bearing it alone.

'Nothing can shock you? Really?'

'Really.'

'I'm pretty sure I can shock you.'

Egged on by drink, I'm getting more and more adventurous. I know I'm playing with fire, but some strange instinct is urging me to trust him. He doesn't say anything for a while, as if trying to think how to reply. He can tell that, whatever I'm thinking of confessing, I'm still hesitating.

'If you're sure you want to, I'll listen,' he says.

He can tell I can't quite make up my mind. Revealing my hidden life would mean trusting him completely and counting on his loyalty to keep the secret. But I don't know him. How and why can I trust him? I look at him searchingly and know he won't say anything. Still, there's a glimmer of lucidity left in me which stops me going further.

'Don't worry. It'll stay between you and me. I can swear it.'

So I throw myself in. I turn the words round and round inside my head to find an appropriate verbal construction for them, because I've never said them out loud.

'Do you know where I was last week?'

He shakes his head. He can't possibly know.

'I was with a fifty-year-old man who paid me to touch my body. I'm a prostitute.'

I've spat it all out without thinking. Once I've actually done it I back away slightly as if it was someone else talking.

For a second his eyes probe mine even more keenly and the upper part of his face screws up but, remembering his promise, he's quick to adopt what he hopes is a neutral expression.

'I see,' he says simply.

He doesn't lay a hand on my shoulder, doesn't make a single compassionate gesture which would exasperate me. No, he just wants to understand and asks me loads of questions. The rest of the night carries on like the beginning; my revelation hasn't done anything to ruin the evening, quite the opposite – it's brought us closer.

Paul eventually breaks the spell which has lasted about six hours. Six consecutive hours when there was nothing in the world but the two of us. I really didn't notice the time passing and I think Paul must be joking when he comes over with the floor mop, having a clean-up before closing time.

'You're going to have to move on, we're closing!'

The two of us burst out laughing, both realising we've lost all track of time. Olivier gets up and holds out his hand to me, to take me outside. Drunk and giggling, I give Paul a quick wave goodbye. When we get outside, Olivier walks me home, holding me up by the waist because I'm zigzagging all over the place. Both of us laugh hysterically all the way, under the effects of excess alcohol. Outside my door he makes sure I've got my keys and can open the door all right. Then, slowly and gently, he kisses my cheek.

I smile at him and go up to the apartment to fall asleep alone. But happy.

Chapter 16

Clambering

4 February 2007

MY BIRTHDAY'S GETTING CLOSER by the minute. I'm going to be nineteen. 'A wonderful age,' everyone always says. I'm not really fussed what number it says on the dial.

Nineteen years old. Two relationships (one of which is on-going), a literature Baccalaureate under my belt, a year at uni which is turning out better than expected and a hidden life as a prostitute. Not bad at just nineteen. Only nineteen years have passed, but I feel ten years older than that.

I'm nearly nineteen and still just as desperately short of money. The balance sheets don't look good, far from it. My tiny mobile phone package has been withdrawn by my service provider. I've got financial priorities, like my rent, that I'm struggling to meet, and most of the time I don't buy a ticket when I take the Métro to uni because I can't afford the luxury of a travel card.

I try to look on the bright side of things. I love my course. It's four months now since I joined the huge student body, and I couldn't be happier about it. Even when I'm tired, I go to lectures gladly, very conscious of the opportunity I'm getting to study (almost) for free. I'm still just as eager to learn and I'm sure I've found my niche with modern languages. My tutors are very encouraging and one of them even admitted recently that he could see me as a future high-flyer in language teaching.

On top of that, I've had the results from my exams in January. I passed them all with an average of 75 per cent! I couldn't believe it when I got my marks through the post. So there is some justice in the world; I didn't do all that work for nothing.

My limited budget obviously means I can't buy all the books I need, so the library has become one of my favourite places. I like browsing there and killing time over the more precious volumes. But it's not particularly big and it's often been raided before I get there, at least the books I need for my course have gone. Still, these recurring inconveniences don't knock any of the innate enthusiasm out of me, they just slow down the learning process a bit. I'm envious of students who go straight to the local bookshop to order books in the original language and hand over their credit cards with a serene smile.

I'm also desperate to have my own laptop because they're becoming well and truly indispensable. The idea first came to me one day with the telesales company. Someone who worked there told us all there was going to be a prize draw and the top prize was a laptop. You can imagine my reaction to this news. I took up residence on internet sites for computers as soon as I had a spare moment and drooled over the latest technological marvels. I chose my theoretical favourite, knowing full well my parents would never be able to afford to give me one, even for my birthday.

I feel helpless when I think of my everyday expenses. It was over a month ago that I had that first meeting with Joe. In that time, I've had three big customers who temporarily fished me out of the red by giving me over 600 euros between them. Thanks to them, I settled my major financial problems, the ones that had been building up for a while, but there's still the rent, bills etc. It's endless. Too many things to think about and pay for. I feel swamped.

I go back to my ads on the internet.

First I contact an amateur photographer ... who makes me wear the most improbable outfits. Even in my most outrageous fantasies I couldn't think up things like that. As the session goes on I find him more and more dubious. He gets demanding, almost aggressive in the way he speaks to me if I don't do what he wants.

'Oh, come on, Laura, don't stand like that! Do you really think you're going to turn anyone on in that position? Don't be such a lump! It needs to be sexier, yes, like that, with your mouth open, good!'

I bring the shoot to an end as soon as I can. When I pocket the money I realise it's not as much as I can get from sleeping with a stranger. And, anyway, I'm not at all comfortable with the idea: photos leave a trail. I'm not prepared to take that sort of risk. I'm keen to stay as discreet as possible. The guy calls me back several times, even suggests threesomes with another girl.

'It's OK, she's a student like you, you'll get on really well, I know you will!'

Just the thought of ending up with some other poor girl in the same shitty situation as myself makes my blood run cold. He can tell I'm hanging back so he raises the fee, going higher and higher till he's quoting sums that seem unbelievable to someone like me. All the same, I get this feeling that if I accept the offer I'll fall into his clutches. He's got every characteristic of the classic pimp: cajoling and protective one minute, violent the next. He seems to be part of a network that operates all over V. If I let him get close to me, I'll never get out of prostitution. I can't see this as my future – not that any prostitute can, mind you.

The fact that I've come so close to the downward spiral of networks like that makes me shudder. I feel weak and powerless in their manipulative hands but at the same time strong for keeping my head screwed on. So far I've succeeded in spotting danger in time and haven't just accepted any old thing. I've managed to avoid pimps, but how long can I hold out? Once you become a prostitute you can't help being in a world where people know you and recognise you. I haven't got any money and it feels as if the deeper I go into this hidden life, the more trouble I have making ends meet. With every new financial crisis I'm tempted to turn to prostitution. It's a vicious circle, scoffing at me and dragging me down like quicksand: the more money I earn, the more I spend and the more I want.

I do know that I've been 'lucky' so far. No one has forced me and I haven't landed up with any nutcases. I shake at the thought that I may actually be waiting for something more shocking to happen before I put an end to this double life. And what if that catalytic event never happens? What if the limits are pushed back bit by bit, so gradually that I don't see the danger coming? Will I be one of the so-called 'professionals' one day? Will I have the strength to get back out?

I only let myself think like that very occasionally. Not that I'm in denial: I'm perfectly aware that I'm playing with fire. I'm just trying to protect myself. At the moment I haven't found any other way of getting money quickly, so I might just as well try not to weigh myself down too much with what I'm doing.

All this self-destructive introspection is feeding my schizophrenia. I can feel two different versions of me emerging while I think. I'm not all black or all white; I'm not completely a prostitute or completely a student – every aspect of my life's a contradiction. The rest of the time I believe firmly in the future. I can see myself with a little family in a beautiful house, doing a job I love, far removed from all this crap. I know I've got the resources to clamber back out of the hole. I'll get through this, of course I will. Later I'll always have a secret sense of having succeeded, of victory. Where few girls have triumphed, I'll serve as an example.

Later, I've made up my mind, I'll be a good person. Right now I can't afford to be.

I've started thinking more and more seriously about the Joe solution. Since we met the first time he hasn't left me alone. I get emails from him every day and I delete them automatically without even reading them. As a newcomer to the profession, I can't contemplate seeing the same customers again. But I'm quickly coming to realise that regulars are exactly the people I need to rely on because they really are a safety net for us in our trickiest times – 'us' being prostitutes.

I think I'm stupidly hoping for a *Pretty Woman* scenario with a Richard Gere lookalike coming along and taking me away from all this hell. Although I do remind myself that's not going to happen if I keep seeing the same customers. So I'm looking further afield for my rare pearl, avoiding Joe like the plague. I can't help smiling when I think that, even with a customer, I'm dreaming of a sort of Prince Charming.

But this Richard Gere is taking his time and when I get yet another letter from my landlady saying I must pay the rent by the end of the week, I tell myself I can easily find customers all over the place. Customers I know I can trust are not so easy. The ads often ooze with rampant perversity which stops me replying to them. Joe's different. The lasting impression I have of him is that I took him for a ride. He was quite happy to pay me for virtually nothing: just rubbing his hands over my body a bit. For now his fantasies strike me as perfectly manageable. I've forgotten the horrible feelings I had while I was with him, all the embarrassment and disgust I felt. I haven't yet worked out that that's exactly where the danger lies: only remembering the envelope full of money.

My landlady's letter is followed the next day by my payslip. I smirk at the sight of my salary: peanuts, that's what I'm earning with those phone calls.

I contact Joe that same evening, from a cyber-café, initially just asking him how he is. The poor bloke must live in front of his computer because he answers within seconds.

In the very next email I tell him it's OK to meet up in the next few days, and the sooner the better because I need money in a hurry. He seems eager to agree, urged on by his desire. But, being polite, he does still ask how I am. I slip the fact that it's nearly my birthday into my reply, and suggest we could meet up on the day. Without a moment's hesitation I send the page about my dream laptop as an attachment.

I know many people will find that shocking. I feel that if these perverts want to have me, then they can pay a high price to get me. Even so, I still can't get used to the idea that I'm a 'prostitute'. I feel as if I'm worth more than that. And money is the only way I can find to prove it to myself. I'm going to be nineteen and, this year more than any other, I need support and reassurance. I have this stupid idea I'll get that from a computer given to me by a customer. God, I can be thick!

His next email doesn't come so quickly. I can tell I've unsettled him a bit. But how could he begin to think I've got back in touch with him because I like him? The only thing I'm interested in is his money. Still, he does answer by asking why I need a computer. I explain that having one would make my everyday life as a student much easier. I lay it on a bit thick with the treacly details because I know I'm dealing with a protective daddy who's quite easy to soften up. I get his reply a few minutes later:

Laura,

It seems times are pretty hard for you at the moment, and I can quite see how badly you need a computer. Which model are you interested in? Do you have any particular preferences? . . .

I instantly know that it's in the bag. I'm not even ashamed of myself. Right now I think I would accept anything from him because I'm convinced that our next meeting will be my last experience as a prostitute.

He takes the lead and arranges to meet in three days' time. The actual day of my birthday.

Chapter 17

Falling

7 *February 2007*

IT'S ONE O'CLOCK and I'm waiting for him outside the same hotel as the first time. We're going to spend two hours together because I have to go to work afterwards. The episode with Pierre is fresh in my mind and my eyes are darting frantically in every direction. I try to watch everyone who passes without being spotted myself, hoping Joe will get here soon. Ironically, I will only feel comfortable when I'm alone with him in the room. I know that no passers-by who see us together in the street would be duped.

I once talked to a prostitute without actually revealing my own shady activities to her and she told me that when she's waiting on a pavement she stays in touch with her 'colleagues' every half-hour by mobile phone. The minute one of them gets into a car she lets all the others know so that they can take action if they don't see her come back safely. Students, who operate mostly via the internet, are definitely exposed to much more danger alone in a room than standing on a pavement.

I see him in the distance, still armed with his magician's briefcase. We give each other a kiss hello and he says, 'Go up to the room ahead of me.'

'Why?'

'Because of last time with those policemen, I'd rather we tried to be more discreet. You never know. Ask for the key at reception. I didn't know your surname so I gave them mine.'

Of course he doesn't know my surname. And there's no way he ever will.

'Then go up and make yourself comfortable. I'll be up shortly.'

By 'make yourself comfortable' he means put on the sexy clothes he's asked me to bring. I nod and head over to reception. The young woman at the desk looks up at me with a professional smile on her face.

When I get to the room I listen to see if there are any sounds coming from inside. I'm convinced I can hear moaning, I'm getting suspicious now. Someone might be waiting for me and might want to hurt me. I literally flatten my ear against the white wood of the door. Nothing: so I conclude that my endless imagination is playing tricks on me, and I must stop being so paranoid. I turn the key in the lock.

When I open the door the first thing that greets me are the green curtains. Just like the first time I'm struck by how ugly they are. This room is definitely smaller but the décor is identical, so it feels more or less the same. Nothing much has changed so far and I find that strangely reassuring.

I notice a laptop sitting on a table opposite the bed. There's a porn film playing on the screen and I'm relieved to discover I wasn't dreaming: that's where the moaning is coming from. There's a note on the bed. Another thing that hasn't changed about Joe. Leaving letters for his expensive lovers is clearly one of his fantasies.

> *Laura,*
>
> *I'm very happy to be seeing you again today. I'd like you to start by having a shower. Then I will come and knock on the door three times. I want you to say, 'Come in, master.'*
>
> *After that I'd like you to lie down on the bed. I want you to say, 'Hello, master, everything you see here is yours.'*

How ridiculous! He's stepped up his domination fantasies. I'm starting to feel frightened. The mood of this session is breaking away from last time – Joe kept things more at arm's length then.

At no point does the letter mention the computer. Just this once, Laura, and it'll be the last, I tell myself.

I go over to the machine slowly, to have a look at it. I'm beginning to wonder whether it's for me or if Joe just wants to thumb his nose at me. I feel he could do either. I finger the keyboard gently, longing for it but still wondering whether I'm really prepared to do anything to have it. And what if this laptop isn't for me? What if he decides not to give it to me at the end? My whole mind revolves round the thought of owning it, my wanting it has become an immeasurable need. I want this laptop whatever it costs me.

I decide to go and have a shower to get things straight inside my head. There's a nice surprise waiting for me in the bathroom: there isn't a mirror. I don't think I would have coped with seeing myself today; on my nineteenth birthday preparing to sell my body for the sake of a computer. I have a quick shower and I'm still drying myself when I hear Joe bang on the door. I go over to the middle of the room, naked, and say, 'Come in, master.'

I can't help laughing when I hear myself saying these words. I can picture him grinning with delight on the other side of the door. Instead, he comes in and stares at me for a few seconds before saying curtly, 'We won't have any giggling.'

He must feel that, given his generous present, he can afford to be more demanding with me. Come on, sweetheart, I think to myself, don't try to be too clever today. Play the game, there's a laptop at stake . . . I'm really obsessed with the thing.

'Lie down,' Joe says, interrupting my thoughts, 'so that you're across the width of the bed and on your stomach.'

I do as I'm told without any resistance, not even daring to open my mouth to speak. In this position, Joe can see my body clearly, especially my buttocks which I loathe.

It's the middle of the day and the light's coming straight through the green curtains – which is hardly surprising, given the state they're in. I really don't feel comfortable.

My body is longer than the bed is wide so my head and feet hang over the sides. Joe notices this and says, 'Let your head drop down and put your hands under the bed.'

I do as he says, although I can't really see where he's going with this. I just hope he's not going to ask me to put my left leg on my head or do a headstand! I can feel the cold edge of a cardboard box under the bed. I pull it towards me to get it out of its hiding place and have a look at it.

A laptop. My laptop. I can't help smiling when I see it. My mind's suddenly whirring manically. Now that I've got my present, why should I sleep with him? But how could I think for a minute Joe would let me get away with that?

He's not that stupid. He must have seen the glimmer of malice in my eye because he suddenly says, 'Of course you can open it afterwards.'

So I'll have to go through with this; there's no escape. I've just grasped that he's also going to pay me for today. I smile at the thought of these future riches. I'm also feeling genuinely emotional: this computer's the most expensive present anyone's ever given me. I haven't been given much in life without something being expected in return. Obviously, Joe gives me something in financial terms but I've now had a glimpse of another aspect of his personality which I didn't know about till today: his human side, his generosity. At least, that's what I tell myself.

The vicious circle has begun: he's manipulating me but I don't realise he is. Joe knows what he's doing. He wants me and knows he needs to impress me with money. The boundaries between us have been pushed back further. Joe's in the driving seat.

He asks me to sit on the bed, beside him. The film on the computer has been on pause and now he turns up the volume. It's an amateur sadomasochistic film featuring a naked woman – fortyish and slightly plump – being burned with a candle. She's tied to the chair she's sitting on, there's wax trickling between her breasts and she's screaming for her life. The more she screams, the more the cruel bastard responsible for her suffering enjoys it. She seems to be enjoying it too, in fact. The images flit before my eyes without making an impression on my retina; I actually find it really hard to watch the scene.

I quite often watch porn films: out of curiosity with girlfriends or to heighten arousal with a boy, like everyone. But sadomasochistic stuff is totally different. I don't think I'll ever grasp the appeal of that sort of film. After a couple of minutes I can't stand the scene any longer and have to look away. I've turned to stone watching those images. Joe, on the other hand, absolutely loves them.

'Honestly, Joe, I can't watch this. It's just not my thing.'

'The problem is that it is my thing, but I won't ask you to watch.'

His tone of voice is radically different from last time. He sounds full of contempt for me. I've slipped to the ranks of the lowliest whore, only here to spread her legs and shut her mouth.

'What I want to suggest is that you tie your hands to the bed.'

I immediately make the connection with the video. Does he want to burn me too? And there I was thinking I was safer with him in a hotel room! Joe softens slightly.

'Don't worry, Laura.'

He moves closer to me gently, then leans my body slowly backwards till I'm lying down, before turning me onto my side. Next he brings my hands together behind my back and ties them together with my jumper which is lying on the bed. The knot isn't very tight which I do find quite reassuring – I could break free if I wanted to.

Joe doesn't seem inclined to leave that option open for me. He produces a piece of cord from nowhere and ties my ankles, also behind my back. Then, as a security measure, he ties my feet and wrists together. I must look like a slab of cold meat on a butcher's block. Why am I letting him do this to me?

Now he takes a dildo from his briefcase. It's not the first time I've seen a real one, but this looks bigger. At the sight of the thing, I shudder and give a little whimper of fear. Joe doesn't react. He couldn't really care, now that I'm tied up.

Captive. I'm at his fucking mercy now.

He comes over to me and puts a screwed-up tissue in my mouth, then completes the effect with a blindfold round my head. In a couple of minutes he's succeeded in immobilising me and silencing me, and I haven't had a chance to react. I feel powerless and just keep thinking in terror, Even if he hurts me I can't scream.

With the help of lubricant and his artificial toy, Joe manages to arouse me physically. Then comes the horror and suffering. The first thrust is indescribably painful.

I scream but it stays muffled inside the tissue. He doesn't stop, oh no, quite the opposite. I'm bellowing 'Stop,' inaudibly and the tears are streaming down my face because the pain is so unbearable. I clamp my thighs together as best I can to make him understand he's got to stop. I writhe furiously so that he now can't get anything inside me, try as he might. And anyway, my wails must be becoming audible from outside. Panicking at my desperation, he finally unties the blindfold and the cord, setting me free once more. As soon as the last knot is undone, I jump to my feet and turn slowly to face him, my hair all over the place, still gasping for breath – I must look like one of the Furies. I look him right in the eye. I could kill him.

He just looks at me rather sheepishly, perfectly aware of how I feel. But, yet again, he seems to like the situation. Looking at my red, bloodshot eyes, he says, 'What's the matter? I thought that was what you liked, being submissive.'

Even he doesn't believe it. I don't say anything but snatch up my clothes and start getting dressed as quickly as I can. Who knows what else he could do! I've seen enough for today. For ever, actually.

'Are you leaving? We agreed on two hours. You've still got another hour to spend with me.'

Afraid that he might get violent, I decide to invent an excuse. He probably won't believe it but who cares, I've got to get out of here. With shaking hands, I find the strength to mumble unintelligibly quickly, 'It's my birthday today so I'm not actually going to work. My friends are waiting for me in a café to celebrate over a drink. I'm halfway through exams as well, so I won't be able to spend long with them, because I've got to get home to revise afterwards.'

I spew out as many excuses as possible, thinking that in amongst all those lies there must be one that will do the job. I can feel my mind and body on the brink of a panic attack. I've got to get out quickly before I go mad in here, in this tacky hotel room. Money or no money, I'm getting out of the place.

Joe then uses the last argument that might mollify me enough to stay a bit longer. He plays the excuses card too. 'You mustn't take it like that, Laura. It was just a little fantasy.'

'A little fantasy? Well, it's absolutely not my idea of one.'

I stop at that, seeing no point in saying anything else. I'm now completely dressed and I'm just putting my coat on when Joe says, 'Aren't you going to shower?'

'No, I'm leaving,' I snap.

I've broken several of his instructions in one go and it's put him off his stride, he doesn't know how to react. I certainly don't want to give him time to think about it, I've already got my hand on the door handle. I retrace my steps for a moment, aware that I've forgotten something. Without even looking at him, I grab the laptop and put it under my arm before running out of the room as quickly as I can.

Joe catches up with me in the corridor.

'Here, Laura, you forgot this too,' he says, handing me an envelope. The same as last time. I open it . . . to find 400 euros inside. He brings his hand to my face as I look up at him. My features are more strained than ever.

'It was good,' he says stroking my hair, 'I liked it.'

He says it with a 'there's a good girl' intonation which makes me feel sick again. I basically rip the envelope from his hand and escape without a backward glance.

I run breathlessly out of the hotel. There are tears streaming down my cheeks and they almost turn to ice in the freezing winter air. I just can't be alone so I go straight to my favourite bar, the one that welcomed me that first time, all those weeks ago, when I didn't feel like going home.

Paul is there, behind the bar, wiping his hundredth glass of the day. He sees me scramble in, cheeks pink with cold, eyes shining. I don't intend to confide in him with my problems (no one must ever know anything), but I don't look my normal self so he won't believe me if I say everything's fine. My face betrays seriously strong emotions; the only way to get out of this is to claim that they're positive.

'Laura? Is everything OK?' he asks as I sit on a barstool.

'Yes, more than OK. Something incredible's just happened to me!' Now there I'm not lying. *Think of something, quick.* 'I've just won this laptop at work. Would you believe it!'

A brilliant explanation! I've coped well. I display my hard-won prize and privately award myself the pennant for the best liar of the year. I order him a coffee and don't even have to ask before he starts telling me all the latest local gossip. Perfect – talking or thinking would have been very hard work the way I'm feeling at the moment.

After a few minutes I interrupt him: 'Hey, Paul, would you mind if I took a shower?'

'No, not at all, make yourself at home.'

I can't sit here a minute longer with Joe's smell on my skin, and now that I've got an opportunity to wash I jump at the chance. I head towards the back of the bar to go upstairs to the bathroom, with the laptop still under my arm. I've got filth and shame deeply imbedded in me, it will take a lot of scrubbing to get them out.

I let the water flow over me for a long time and use half the bottle of shower gel. When I step out I still feel just as dirty but suddenly everything changes: I see the computer sitting in the corner of the room and something extraordinary happens, something I could never have anticipated a moment earlier – I smile. I'm just happy knowing it's now mine. That happiness gets the upper hand and all the fears I felt as I left the hotel flitter away. I feel light and free, ready to face life again. And anyway, it's my birthday and I don't want to ruin the day with gloomy thoughts. I've got plenty of time to mope later. I would never have guessed I'd be smiling this afternoon.

I gather up my things, wave goodbye to Paul and leave the bar, apparently perfectly at ease with myself as I head for work. I can't even see anything wrong with being happy the laptop is mine.

Happy birthday, Laura.

Chapter 18

Love

March 2007

WITHOUT REACHING ANY concrete agreement, Olivier and I have gone on seeing each other alongside my forbidden extra-curricular activities. We've been carried along by our platonic relationship. At least, we're not officially a couple. To calm my own impatience, I try to persuade myself I prefer it like this. We're both afraid of what might happen if we attempt a kiss. We meet up after my work several times a week, very often in Paul's bar where we first met.

I don't know how he makes his living because he always seems to be free to see me and is often the one who suggests we meet. I think he must be unemployed. I can't help making comparisons with my ex-boyfriend Manu. I've gone from someone tight-fisted to someone who may not have much money but asks me out for supper the minute he can afford it. Even before we've taken the step of kissing, I know he's an important part of my life.

We never talk about my clandestine profession as a problem that needs solving. Olivier seems to have accepted the idea that he's interested in a girl who sells her body to pay her way through uni. I have to admit I lost track long ago of exactly how I feel about that aspect of my life. Olivier doesn't ask about it either. He's probably got his own demons to overcome before he feels up to tackling mine.

We spend whole days together, wandering round V, or long evenings at my apartment, chatting till dawn. We get along so easily. Sometimes we disagree but our relationship is unbelievably compassionate: we'll always try to understand what the other is thinking before criticising. We have a lot of fun too. I absolutely love his laugh: seeing and hearing it. Just before he bursts out laughing I can see it about to spring out of his mouth as he draws his lips back into a grin and then succumbs completely. I sit there watching and even forget to laugh myself because I'm so captivated by the sight of him. He's not good-looking but in my eyes he's fantastic. Far from perfect, but that's exactly what gives him a sort of nobility. Then he might stop joking and laughing just to look at me, and we sit in silence together, a beautiful comfortable silence.

I still can't get over how quickly we became so close. I don't waste time looking for explanations, you can't always explain life or how it throws people together. I've often done this, letting events carry me along, taking them in my stride and trying my best not to complain.

One evening he calls to invite me to supper at his house. I accept gladly because being with him is becoming a more and more essential part of my life; I literally miss him the minute we're apart.

We spend a fun, happy evening, nothing unusual about that. We're glad to be together again even though we only saw each other the day before. The conversation follows its usual meandering course through noisy joking and nonsense interspersed with more meaningful subjects. Then, at the end of the meal, Olivier picks up his glass of red wine and clinks his knife on the side of his plate to call for silence. He looks quite serious and I haven't really seen him like this before so I straighten slightly in my chair.

'Laura . . .'

He's still piecing his words together. Is that a good thing? I don't say anything, no point.

'Laura . . .'

Then he gets up and gently kisses me. It's the most beautiful declaration of love I've ever had. The last few months I've heard my own name distorted by the furious urges of total strangers so many times . . . I've even wished I'd never hear it again because it's pushing my schizophrenia to such heights, forcing me to juggle with my new imaginary friend, the room-mate inside my head: Laura the prostitute.

But right now my whole identity is back in its usual place, being who it's meant to be. To him, I'm not a tart, I'm Laura. That kiss confirms the thing we haven't been able to admit to ourselves all these weeks: we're passionately in love. After Manu I would never have guessed I could fall in love again so quickly, bearing in mind my hidden life. Obviously I don't have any feelings for my customers so it's as if I've become hermetically sealed against emotion. Olivier is proving me wrong this evening. With that kiss, which might seem insignificant to other people, I feel I'm coming back to life, I can accept myself as a living, loving human being and not just an object at the disposal of strangers.

The next few weeks are the most intense of my short life. Olivier and I are inseparable now, we take life on together, not stopping to think about the future. I carry on seeing customers for the simple reason that I still need money. I've become increasingly demanding in my own way of life, treating myself to things I would never have dreamed of having six months ago.

The first time we make love something very telling happens. In the heat of the action Olivier stops and looks right at me with those green eyes. He breaks the silence and says, 'Laura . . .' He swallows hard, as if summoning the courage to speak. 'Laura, what are you doing?'

'Um, I'm here with you. We're making love.'

'No, Laura. What you're doing is letting me fuck you, it's not the same thing.'

I recoil for a moment.

'*I*'m not fucking *you*, Laura. I'm making love to you.'

I stop completely to think about what Olivier's said for a moment. After months of having no sex life except with customers, I haven't noticed that I've developed various reflexes to protect myself. Waiting, not moving, closing my eyes: obviously none of that is compatible with a lover.

Olivier holds me in his arms for a long time and I fall into a deep, peaceful, serene sleep. The next morning we make love wonderfully gently.

Olivier doesn't turn a blind eye to my forbidden life, quite the opposite. Over the weeks he's become my appointments diary: I always tell him where and when I'm meeting someone in case something happens to me. I never stop to think how bizarre this relationship is. He's literally giving me permission to cheat on him and, worse than that, helping me organise it. We don't mention a rendezvous again afterwards because he doesn't need to hear what's happened. I don't think of him as being masochistic and don't see myself as sadistic. We just want to share everything and if that means he needs to know my customers' names and when I'm meeting them then I'm prepared to talk to him about them.

One day I arrange to meet a new customer near the station towards the end of the afternoon. Before going to the rendezvous, Olivier and I nip into Paul's bar for a coffee. As I take the first scalding mouthful of coffee my mobile rings. It's the man in question on the phone.

'Laura? I'd rather meet you at the car park in front of the station at about nine this evening, is that OK? I know that's later than planned, but something's come up this afternoon.'

'In front of the station? I'm not sure,' I say, sensing something suspicious about the guy now. 'I'm really not sure. I can't say I'm happy about meeting there at that time of night.'

Olivier has looked up and is listening to the conversation.

'No, no, don't worry, Laura. I'll be in a car. I'll pick you up and we'll drive off straight away. We won't spend the evening there.'

I need to end this conversation right away and cancel this rendezvous. There's no way I'm meeting a stranger in a car by the station that late in the evening.

'I'm going to have to cancel, I'm not free then.'

I cut him off without waiting for a reply. Olivier hasn't stopped looking at me, but I avoid catching his eye. He can tell something's not right.

'Is everything OK?' he asks eventually.

'Yes, everything's fine. I've cancelled a customer.'

He doesn't even have time to smile before my mobile rings again. I should have expected this, the weirdo won't give up that easily. We contemplate the shrill ring tone. We know who's calling and, for the first time in our relationship, I can tell that my illegal activities have come between us.

I pick up. Him again.

'Laura, why did you hang up? I'm sure we can meet up later, or another day. I mean, we can come to some arrangement, can't we?'

I mumble that I'm not free and snap my mobile shut again. Olivier's eyes are glowing with rage, he's about to explode. I take both his hands and cover them with kisses. We both feel the pressure of the situation, waiting for the phone to ring again inevitably.

And yes, the silence is broken a few minutes later. With an incredibly violent swipe, Olivier snatches the phone, flips it open and barks 'Hello!' furiously.

I have no idea what the customer says. I imagine he's frightened to hear the loathing in this male voice. All I can do is watch Olivier bellowing at the guy never to call me again, and saying he personally will track him down if he tries to contact me again.

I realise that we've overstepped our boundaries. By getting carried away and shouting and losing track of what he's saying, Olivier has unleashed the anger he's been accumulating – unconsciously or not – over the last weeks.

After several seconds of insults he slams the phone down on the wooden table. He looks at me for a split second then looks away and concentrates on his coffee. We never discuss the subject again and I keep my prostitution a secret. No more diary keeping, no more joint scheduling, I'm back to being his girlfriend and he decides to turn a blind eye once more on things he should never have known.

Our passionate relationship is very soon soured by this episode. Olivier can't pretend any longer, while I just can't stop now: I always want more money. At this point in my life losing Olivier would be the scariest thing in the world but I still go on seeing customers. Prostitution is part of my daily life now and I persuade myself I'd never cope financially without it.

One morning I wake up in his apartment and find his side of the bed empty. The sheets are still warm and it's very early in the morning. Olivier is in the kitchen, standing by the window deep in thought. He's drinking his coffee slowly, his expression blank.

I tiptoe over to him and put my hand over his back lovingly. He doesn't react. Then the thing I've been dreading for several days happens.

'Laura . . .'

Always that same 'Laura', the same as when he declared his love for me and helped me find my own identity again. But this time it sounds horribly different. This 'Laura' is a full stop, this 'Laura' brings an end to our relationship, here in this gloomy kitchen in the dawn light.

That's it. I leave the same day, packing away my stuff scattered about in the pandemonium of his apartment. I only let the tears flow when I'm outside. For once I don't even try to wipe them away, they deserve to be there.

Chapter 19

Panic

25 March 2007

I'M LEANING UP AT the counter in Paul's bar, making easy, superficial chit-chat. I haven't been back since splitting up with Olivier a week ago. And he's making a point of avoiding the place too.

For the first time in my life I feel alone in the world. I made a choice a few months ago to share my weighty secret and now it's like I no longer have the strength to bury it deep inside me like I did before. It weighs too heavily on me.

Paul is tactful enough not to mention Olivier: perhaps out of respect for our unspoken suffering. Perhaps also because he couldn't care less. So we've reverted quite spontaneously to easygoing meaningless conversations.

This afternoon I've made up my mind to come out after spending a week mulling over my pain alone in my apartment, buried in coursework. I know I've got to forget and move on but it's much harder that I thought. I owe it to myself to get back to my 'normal' life, even though I can't bring myself to see it like that.

All of a sudden the door opens. It's not a very big bar and when people come in they can't help being eyed by customers inside.

I recognise him straight away. My blood runs cold, I'm terrified. He's with his girlfriend, who may well be his wife and, horror of horrors, his child's here too. A smiley blond little boy with big blue eyes and gorgeous curls. I give his wife a quick glance – I can't resist it, I need to see what she looks like. She's quite tall, dark-haired, a bit chubby but very elegant. She's holding the child's hand and smiling at him. She must be a good mother.

I turn back to the bar quickly, with my back to the door. I can't think what to do.

'Hello there, Paul,' says the man.

'Hello, Mathias! How are you? It's been ages and, look, you've brought the whole family today.'

Shit, they know each other. What a nightmare! A month ago this bloke contacted me for a 'massage' in a seedy hotel. And here he is now in a bar, *my* bar. I don't dare move from my barstool, mainly so I don't have to face him, obviously, but also so I don't have to acknowledge what's happening.

Mathias hasn't actually noticed me yet and starts chatting to Paul while Goldilocks babbles away to his mother behind me. The man has only seen me once so it's perfectly legitimate for him not to recognise the back of my neck. After all, I'm just a pleasant mistake he soon forgot, but I remember them all. I know their faces by heart because I've had plenty of time to look at them. I recognise their voices and often turn round in the street when I think I hear one of them.

He's literally right next to me at the bar now, rubbing shoulders with me. I've got to get out of here, leave this bar as quickly as I can. I get off my stool with my head down and, as I put my feet to the ground, I nearly trip over my bag, which makes him look round.

Our eyes meet. He half opens his mouth. He knows he's seen me somewhere and, after racking his brain for a minute, remembers where. I can read the horror and panic in his eyes. We freeze for a split second but it feels like an eternity.

'Are you leaving already, Laura?' Paul asks when he sees me picking up my bag and heading for the door. 'You haven't even finished your coffee.'

'I've just remembered I'm meant to be somewhere, I've got to go,' I stammer, getting tangled in the strap of my bag.

'Hang on a minute. Here, this is Mathias, one of my best friends.'

No, I already know your friend . . . rather well, in fact. Paul can't possibly understand the turmoil I'm in at the moment. If he touched my clammy hands he'd know something strange was going on. Mathias, meanwhile, is frantically glancing at his beloved who's crouching behind him and – thank God – is far too preoccupied playing with her offspring.

'Hello, pleased to meet you, I'm Laura,' I say, holding out my hand for him to shake.

'Err, hi, err . . . Mathias, pleased to meet you.'

Oh Christ! Our fingers are stiff and wooden as they come together in a fleeting pretence of a handshake. Our eyes dart about anxiously looking for some sort of distraction. Paul notices our embarrassment.

'Are you OK, Laura? Don't you want to stay a bit longer?'

'No, I've got to go, sorry.'

And I really, really am sorry. Without another word I head for the door, mumbling an inaudible 'Goodbye.' I can see Paul watching me, baffled, then shrugging his shoulders and getting on with drying glasses.

For a couple of minutes I run without stopping to get the bar and the incident out of my mind. I come to a halt on a street corner and take a huge deep breath. This is too much: my two lives have now converged, my two personalities have met. Until now I've managed to keep things apart, but please don't push me too far. I've come face to face with Mathias's family: everything I refuse to picture when I'm with a customer has just materialised today through no fault of my own.

This can't go on any longer. Whatever happens I've got to get away from this city.

Chapter 20

Dispossessed

30 March 2007

I PROMISED MYSELF I'd never see Joe again, but he managed to appeal to me. I told him I was leaving for Paris, stupidly believing that he'd leave me alone then. Was I thinking straight?

'If you're off to Paris, you'll need money. You can't leave with empty pockets. Go on, just once more, it's such a little thing and it does us both a favour.'

He gave me his mobile number recently and he's got mine. I gave it to him under duress and I now realise it was a mistake. It would be lying to say he calls me regularly – he's literally hounding me! He really does like me, I seem to match his fantasy of a sexy flirtatious student.

He's now made a crazy suggestion: nothing less than a thousand euros for five hours. I can't deny it's very tempting, but five hours is a long time. What's he cooking up? I can't help thinking exactly how much money it is. I've never achieved that sort of rate, and a sum like that would certainly make going to Paris easier. I could take my time to find a respectable job I like, instead of grabbing the first offer in some tacky bar. I can't contemplate landing up in the same shit I'm in here. I'm well and truly running away from V. I don't want to have to hide and scheme and lie any more. In Paris I'll be a good girl.

We've arranged to meet at the same hotel as usual. To be honest, I find the place reassuring. In spite of everything and even though I admit it's stupid, I feel a sort of trust in Joe. Yes, he made me scream with pain and humiliation last time we met, but at least I know him and I don't think I'm risking my life by seeing him. I know that whatever he might do to me and however much it makes me cry when I'm alone in my bed afterwards, he won't strangle me or stab me. Basically, he's got me under his control. He pays well.

At first we kept in touch off and on by email. He was quite insistent about arranging to meet again and, reading between the lines, I could feel his raging desire. He constantly suggested times when we could meet and I kept saying I couldn't make it. To pretend I was making an effort, I suggested a meeting too but at a time I knew he wouldn't be free. I often wonder why I played that game, why I didn't just delete him from my mailbox. I can't help myself; I see him as a safety net, someone who can give me a bit of breathing space financially if I run out of money.

And right now that's exactly what's happened. I need money now that I've decided to exile myself, to run away, because I feel my life is toppling dangerously towards something I soon won't be able to control. Obviously, the main problem is still cash. I haven't got any, not even enough for my train ticket.

Mind you, I've got everything organised. A friend of my mother's is going to put me up until I find a job and an apartment. I've managed to get hold of a fake medical certificate giving me permission to skip tutorials at uni. One of my friends is going to copy all her notes for me, and I'll come and take the exams at the end of May. As for my job . . . Well, never mind, I wasn't planning to spend the rest of my life with a telesales company anyway. Friends and family know I'm leaving soon. My father just sighed, finding it easier to ignore me than bollock me. He feels as if he's reliving my last year of school when I walked out on lessons. But there's no way I'm giving up on my course, I'm carrying on by correspondence. Uni represents my only way out of all this, and I'm clinging so desperately to that idea that I'm more motivated than ever to do well.

Basically, this 'exile' is my last chance to break away from prostitution, from getting swamped by it. As soon as I've got the money for that sodding one-way ticket, I'll be off.

But I haven't got the money. Ironically, I need to see Joe again in order to escape my life as a prostitute. So I've given in to his suggestions and in one of my emails

I asked him for his mobile number. After thinking it over for a few days I've called him.

'Joe, it's Laura.'

'Hello, Laura, how are you?'

I don't want any small talk so I cut the conversation short and get straight to why I'm calling.

'Five hours, Joe, and not a minute more. Five hours for a thousand euros.'

He must be surprised that I've got down to business right away, but is quick to reply, 'Err, that's perfect, Laura. Five hours is perfect, and a thousand euros is OK by me. Shall we meet at the hotel as usual? Shall we say one o'clock on Wednesday?'

'Yes, Wednesday's fine. I'll be there.'

'Don't forget to bring some sexy clothes.'

I hang up straight away. He always asks me to come equipped with skimpy provocative clothes because my jeans and T-shirts don't turn him on much, or not enough. What he wants is a student playing at being a grown-up in women's clothes. That's what he likes.

On Wednesday we meet outside the hotel and he asks me to go in first. I can tell he's dreamed up some scenario, and I imagine there's a letter waiting for me on the bed as usual.

Bingo, yes, there's a note on the bed:

Hello, Laura,

I'm very glad you've agreed to come. I'm sure today is going to be perfect.

*As usual, I'd like you to take a shower first. Then
you will go out of the room and come and knock at
the door. When I answer, you can come in.*

These are his normal requests: the shower, the knocking
. . . nothing new there, then. In a way I find it reassuring.
I put the letter back down and go to the bathroom.

So I have my shower, letting the scalding water stream
slowly over my body. I feel lethargic, I haven't got any
energy. I don't think I've got the strength to answer back
today.

When I've washed thoroughly I come back into the
bedroom and find him lying on the bed. Without a word,
I carry on following his instructions and leave the room.
I knock and – again not giving him time to answer
because I'm terrified at the thought of meeting someone
in the corridor – I go back in.

He doesn't move and doesn't speak, just indicates I
should pick up the letter where I left off.

*Today we're going to stay in the room for about
half an hour to talk, then we're going to a place I
want to show you, very close to the hotel.*

A place? What place? Even though this hotel reminds me
of disgusting things, at least I know it. I don't know what
other sort of places Joe might go to, they could be
dangerous. Anyway, I really don't want to end up
outside with him, where everyone can see us. I don't
want to be exposed. My head is weighing things up: on

the one hand it's screaming at me to leave, but on the other the 1,000 euros sit there glittering. This isn't looking good at all.

It's a sex shop I know well. We're going to have fun there and enjoy ourselves.

I look up at him, my eyes full of questions and unspoken fears.

'Here, come and sit next to me on the bed,' he says.

So this is what he calls 'talking'. He's going to trot out all his arguments to persuade me to go to that dismal place with him – I can picture it already.

'Listen, there's nothing wrong with the place, it really turns me on. It's just along the road from the hotel and no one's going to see us on the way there. It's very close by.'

'Joe, I really don't feel like doing this. There'll be people there and I don't want to be seen. I don't feel safe. I really, really don't like the idea. I'd rather stay here.'

'Come on, Laura, don't get upset. It's nice there, there's nothing to worry about, I promise you. No one will see you. There's a room at the back of the shop they keep for regulars. It's very dark in there, no one will see us, you can trust me on that. There are videos we can watch together. It's very exciting. I've been there lots of times with women and everything's always gone well.'

He knows he has to handle me carefully, that I'm bound to refuse. Obviously, I'm not familiar with places like that and the only impression I have of them is grim.

I'm not sure what to expect and that's exactly the problem.

'Listen,' he says after several minutes' silence, 'let's go there and then we'll see. If you really don't feel comfortable we'll come back to the hotel. You know, I completely understand. I'm very shy and discreet too.'

I sigh but a voice inside me whispers, *A thousand euros, Laura, then you can scram. You can leave all this shit behind. Without this money you'll never afford it.*

'OK. But as soon as I want to, we come back,' I eventually agree.

So we head off for the sex shop which really is very near the hotel, on the corner of the street.

As we walk in the doorbell rings and I find myself face to face with the cashier. He's about twenty-five or thirty and so good-looking that I'm rooted to the spot for a minute. Wow! Out on the street, in different circumstances, I might have asked him for his phone number. But here, in this place, with Joe who could easily be my father, I blush furiously.

He's noticed me too. I can tell from his expression, just for a split second, that he likes me, but it soon changes to a look of disgust. He's judging me and must be thinking I'm just some little tart who comes to sex shops to get fucked. He's probably annoyed with himself for liking the look of me for a moment. And, even though I'm a strong character and nothing ever gets the better of me, I admit I feel I've fallen about as low as you can go. This bloke's showing me everything I refuse to see for myself: the image of Laura in her other life, Laura the prostitute who lets dirty old men support her financially. Yup, as far as he's concerned, I'm just a whore. But, hey, he works on the till in a sex shop!

Joe pays our entry, a tiny fee of a few euros, and heads quickly towards the room at the back hidden behind black curtains. Curtains again. They're always there, every time I'm with a customer, confirming that what I'm doing is wrong and dirty. I slip into the room, avoiding eye contact with the employee, who's stopped looking at me anyway.

It's very dark inside and it takes me a few seconds to adjust. The only thing I'm aware of straight away is a strong animal smell, a smell of human flesh. A shudder runs through me. When I eventually make out what's around me I see a big projector on the far side playing a porn film of a crude blonde shrieking with pleasure. About twenty chairs are arranged in rows in front of the screen. At a glance, I'd say there are around ten people in the room, all men, slumped on the chairs or standing masturbating. I have to suppress a groan of disgust. The room's quite big as far as I can make out and it's decorated entirely in black. The overall effect is a bit like a nightclub, and you can tell someone's made an effort to make it look cool, but the effect fails: as soon as you step into the place you know it's intended for dubious activities.

'Here, have a chair,' Joe says. 'We can watch the film together for a bit.'

I'm lost, I can't think what to do now. Sitting down next to these men would give them a chance to see who

I am. What if I know one of them? I haven't got a single viable excuse. Being in a sex shop to choose a DVD just about works, it would give you a reputation as a slightly pervy flirt, but there's no alibi for being seen in this room.

Glum as a six-year-old, I listen to instructions from this man who always assumes a paternal role. I scan for empty spaces that aren't too close to the other men, and sit down in the second row. Joe stays a little way behind, still standing so he can see everything. He watches the other customers and keeps glancing up at the film. I can feel people starting to look at me. I'm the only woman here. They must all be thinking how lucky they are today; they might be able to act out their fantasies with a woman, a real one.

I force myself to watch the film and stop thinking about things, but I just can't. What with the blonde screaming up on the screen and moans of pleasure from these men, I can't shut out the sounds. I don't want to close my eyes. I want to stay in control of myself as much as I possibly can in the circumstances.

Joe comes over to me and, pointing to a man of about fifty, whispers in my ear, 'You can let him get closer. I've mentioned you to him. He won't hurt you, I know him. Him too, he's OK.'

This time he means another man of the same sort of age, sitting in the front row. He points at them quite openly; they're far too busy with their film anyway. So he knows them all and – worse than that – he's told them about me. I can feel a horrible trap closing around me. I was relying on Joe to protect me but he's responsible for my being here. I whisper a quick 'OK' and carry on looking round, as if trying to work out where danger's most likely to strike first.

'That's enough, we've seen enough pictures for today,' Joe says, as if dragging me away from something I love. Actually, given the circumstances, I'd definitely prefer to stay watching this sex film for five hours. I know that when I get up and follow him the serious business will begin. I'm shaking at the thought.

'Did you bring your clothes?' he asks.

'Yes,' I say pointing to the plastic bag I propped up against a wall when we came in.

'Well, go and get changed now. You can use one of those cubicles.'

He gestures towards a cubicle I hadn't noticed behind me. There are three exactly the same along the wall opposite the mini-cinema.

I pick up my things and go in. There's just room for one person, and an ordinary chair is the only furnishing. The white light blinds me slightly when I go in from the almost complete darkness of the main room. I take a skimpy low-cut black nightdress from my bag and change quickly, worried someone might come in and try to touch me. When I look up I realise the cubicle is dotted with little holes at different heights, but I don't grasp what they're for straight away.

I come back out with my arms crossed over my breasts to try to hide some of my flesh. Joe is waiting for me outside and seems rather impressed by what I'm wearing.

I don't usually make much of an effort to bring sexy clothes with me.

'That's great, a very pretty nightie! Right, listen carefully now, you're going to go back into the cubicle and wait for a bit. When you see them you can do whatever you feel like.'

What does he mean 'them'? I don't understand what he's talking about. There's no time to try to work it out: Joe pushes me gently back into the cubicle and closes the door behind me. I sit down on the chair nervously. The next minute a man's penis pokes through one of the holes. So that's what they're for. They'll all be here soon, expecting me to touch them, and more. Where the hell have I landed? I feel so naive for thinking it would all be over quickly.

I can hear moans of pleasure outside. I recoil in disgust and quickly turn the catch on the cubicle door to lock myself in. As I step back, I feel something against my shoulder. Another penis. Then a third, then more. Even if I wanted to I couldn't touch them all, there are so many of them.

The whole absurd set-up suddenly turns my stomach. I put my head in my hands and curl up so I don't have to see them or feel them any more. I'm nothing now, just an object, a wanking machine. This is a nightmare, it can't really be happening. If this is the price I have to pay to get to Paris, then I don't want to go any more. I want to go home straight away.

I look up at the top of the cubicle and see a man's eyes watching me. Only now do I get the full perversity of this contraption. I look away to avoid meeting that probing eye, but come face to face with another. They're all watching me, all wanting me, impatient with longing, for the touch of my hand or my mouth.

I lower my face and wait, with my hands over my ears, shutting out the world. I'm screaming inside. I sing a song to myself in my head to blot out their moaning. I'm heading for a complete breakdown but I'm not even crying. I've got to a level of internal pain so deep that it's way beyond tears.

I don't know how long I stay like this, with my head buried between my knees, but when I look up again the penises have gone. I look round frantically to make absolutely sure. This is so horrible. How long was I curled up like that feeling sorry for myself? Ten minutes? An hour? I can't even begin to make a guess.

Right now I really have to get out of this hellhole, but I'm worried the perverts are waiting outside for me and will throw themselves on me. Still, I can't stay in here for ever. After a moment's hesitation I carefully turn the lock.

To my huge relief, there's no one waiting outside except Joe. He's smiling and looks delighted – he was probably one of the peeping Toms peering at me in the cubicle.

'So, what did you think of it?'

I don't say anything: he knows exactly what I thought of it. I'm freezing and shivering with fear. The most absurd thing about the whole situation is unquestionably the fact that I'm completely dependent on him. There's absolutely no doubt that it was him who asked them to stop. I can see a glint of total power in his eye and there's something about his expression which hints at what's coming next. If I don't do something straight away I'm probably going to end up being taken by all of them. So, with all the energy of despair, I grab my things and try to make a run for it. Joe and the other men look so disappointed. He tries to talk to me but I'm not listening to a word. Half naked and with my things clamped under my arm, I can't get out of the sex shop fast enough.

Joe's behind me already. 'Calm down, Laura, I'll still give you 500 euros.'

I keep losing my balance as I walk, I think I'm going to faint. I feel drugged or drunk. I can't keep myself upright, my legs have given up. I don't have enough survival instinct left to grab the envelope.

We go back to the hotel in silence. I can still smell those men on my body. We don't exchange a single word. I know that if I talk I'll slap Joe or spit in his face. I hate myself for not realising he's just a filthy old man. I want to stop this once and for all. All I can think about now is taking my money and getting away, a long way away. I feel so dirty, I want to cry but I can't even manage that now.

When we get back to the room I tell him, 'I'm not staying. Give me my money now.'

'Go and have your shower. I'll leave the envelope on the bed. We could see each other again on Thursday, what do you think?'

After what he's put me through can he honestly believe I'll agree to see him on Thursday? Even if 500 euros isn't enough to leave for Paris, I never want to see him again. There's no way I'm planning another rendezvous with a perv like him. I'd better not tell him that though. We're alone in the room and, now that I know there are no limits to what he'll do, I don't want to provoke him. He's quite capable of hitting me.

'Yes, we can meet up on Thursday.'

I need to have a shower, I can't stand this smell any longer. Alone in the bathroom I don't give in to the urge to sit on the floor – I know I'd never get back up. I hear the door slam. Joe's left. After scrubbing my skin and hair manically under the burning hot water for quarter of an hour I get dressed again and come out of the bathroom.

There's an envelope waiting for me on the bed, as agreed. I open it, drawn by the money I'm so hoping will compensate for my misery, even just for a moment.

It's got 100 euros in it. I check: just 100 euros. There are 400 euros missing. He tricked me. Tears well up in my eyes, and my first sob turns into a loud wail. I pick up my phone like a banshee and, my eyes clouded with tears, punch out his number so quickly that I have to start again three times, which makes me even angrier. My hands are shaking, I'm screaming like a wild animal and thumping my little fist on the wall. His mobile's not switched on. He must be far away by now.

I turn the envelope upside down and shake it, still hoping to find what I'm owed. Nothing. I even move the desk and shake out the sheets violently. I look around, dazed, trying to convince myself he must have left the rest of my money somewhere in this dump of a room. Absolutely nothing. Instead, there's a letter which he must have put under the envelope before he left.

It's been scribbled down hastily, almost certainly while I was showering.

Laura, as you will have seen, there are only 100 euros in the envelope instead of the 500 I mentioned. I just wanted to be sure I would see you again before you leave for Paris. Trust me, you'll get your money. Enjoy the rest of your day, Laura.

I throw the letter on the floor in a furious temper. I've lost Paris, lost my new life; I'm going to have to stay here. I'll never find a way out, I'm stuck in a rut of prostitution for ever.

The roles are reversed now. Now I'm the one who's been taken for a ride.

Chapter 21

Runaway

12 April 2007

I T'S THURSDAY, I'M BACK outside the hotel, scarcely believing it myself. Needless to say, Joe hasn't shown up. I'm still just as angry, and after half an hour I'm quivering with rage and insulting him under my breath. Passers-by turn to look but I don't notice them; I can only think about one thing at the moment: getting my money.

When I get home I leave an explosive message on his phone which still isn't responding, screaming at him that he'd better call me back to give me my dosh. Not a dickie bird for three days. Three days that I spend moping about my fate, and crying the minute I think of Paris. The Eiffel Tower and all my wonderful plans are collapsing around me.

Finally, my phone rings.

'Laura?'

I recognise his voice straight away. My heart misses a beat.

'Fuck it, Joe, you really pissed me around. I want you to bring me my money right now!' I'm screaming into the phone. Luckily there's no one else in the apartment.

'I know, Laura, I know. Just wait, let me explain –'

'Explain what? You're just a fuckwit. You'd better give me my money straight away.'

'Laura, I'm not at home at the moment. I've had a heart attack, I'm convalescing in the South of France, near Perpignan.'

I interrupt my flow of insults for a minute.

'I wanted to write you a cheque but my wife's frozen my account. I think she suspects something.'

The old Laura would have believed him without a moment's hesitation. The new Laura who was born the day she was caught out, won't fall for this web of lies.

'I don't believe you, Joe, that's not good enough. Give me my money.'

'Laura, I'm telling you the truth, I'm really ill, I've got cancer. I haven't got long to live.'

Those words chill me to the bone. I have to admit I feel a tinge of sadness at the news, despite everything he's done to me. The feeling doesn't last long, though, I hate him again already.

'Listen, Laura,' he goes on, 'I'm leaving here tomorrow. We must see each other again, so I can give you your money. I will give it to you, I promise. And I really want to see you again, too.'

I hang up. I don't believe anything he says now. I'll never believe him again.

Chapter 22

Intrusion

17 April 2007

TWO DAYS AFTER the whole Joe episode, I come home with my arms full of shopping. Just the once won't hurt and I've had enough of scrimping. There's another reason, though: I'm putting up a friend in my apartment and we've decided to treat ourselves to a real feast – tandoori chicken and wild rice. I'd much rather he didn't notice I haven't got any food in the cupboards. We're going to have such a good meal and I'm already drooling at the thought of it. I'm in a really good mood, singing to myself as I struggle with the heavy plastic bags.

When I get in I offload the food in the kitchen and go to find my temporary flatmate.

As we start preparing the meal, he says, 'Oh, by the way, someone tried to get hold of you on the landline a bit earlier. I told him to call back later.'

'Did he give his name?'

'No. Well, he said he was an old friend. Apparently he hasn't heard from you for a long time, so he wanted to know how you were.'

'Well, if it's important he'll call back.'

An hour later, right in the middle of our meal, the phone rings again. I get up to answer it. I recognise his voice straight away. Pierre. The limp businessman. The James Bond in slippers.

'Laura, it's Pierre.'

I take the phone out into the hall. 'How did you get this number?' I ask curtly.

It all suddenly comes back to me: having something to eat, me smoking a cigarette, my bag left open and easy to get into. No need to look for further explanations or try to find out why he's waited so long to get in touch: the net result is he's got my landline number which implies he also has my address. Panic rises up inside me, making my voice sound nervous and laden with threat: 'Don't you ever call me on this number again, do you understand?'

'Yes, but it's your fault. You said you'd get back in touch but you didn't. I want to see you again, Laura.'

The man's mad and I can now see he's been obsessed with me all these months. I completely lose the plot: he could be downstairs right now as we're talking, he might be calling from my street, from inside my building . . .

'Listen, it's very simple: if you don't leave me alone, I'll ring your work and take great pleasure in telling them how partial you are to nineteen-year-old prostitutes. You dare call me again and I'll mess up your life.'

The threat does the trick. There's complete silence on the line, and I hang up before he has a chance to say anything else.

Over the next few days I'm constantly terrified I'll find him downstairs when I go out. I keep turning to look at people in the street, convinced I've seen him in the crowd. I know he hasn't given up because every time I check my answering machine the robotic voice announces how many calls he's made, for example: 'This number has tried to contact you twenty-six times today without leaving a message.' Twenty-six times! What a loser!

One day, when my answering machine has told me for the umpteenth time that Nutcase Pierre has been at it again, I decide to call back the last incoming number. I get some girl who tells me Pierre Thingamebob isn't there and I should ring again in the morning. That means he's making all these calls from work, and now that I know his surname I'm pretty determined to make things difficult for him. Stupid of him. He probably thinks I wouldn't dare pick a fight.

So the next day I calmly dial the number. I have a plan. I get straight through to him. I can feel his face falling apart at the sound of my voice.

'Now you listen to me, Pierre. I just wanted to warn you that if you ever, *ever* try to contact me again, I'll get in touch with the police straight away.'

'Why would you do that?'

'Because when you got hold of my full name you should have checked I wasn't a minor.'

That's knocked the breath out of him. I can hear him saying a stifled 'Shit.' He starts stammering and wheedling, 'Oh, I'm so sorry, Laura, but I just wanted to see you again.'

I've had enough. I've been tricked out of a huge amount of money by Joe and my moving to Paris has suffered for it: I really don't need some stupid jerk of an apathetic businessman pissing me off into the bargain. I start screaming down the phone, pouring out all the hate inside me: 'I'm going to lodge a complaint against you for harassment! I've got your address and your phone number. I know everything about you and I'm going to use it if you try to get to me again!'

'But you're a whore, Laura.'

Fuckwit. He's asked for it, the threats obviously aren't enough. I decide to put my plan into action.

'You don't know prostitutes are protected by the police, then?' I say sardonically.

This isn't actually true of student prostitutes but that doesn't matter, Pierre is far too frightened to check.

'So never again, do you understand, you never call me or email me again, you get out of my life just like you came into it: quickly.'

I hang up on him. I really don't need to wait for his guarantees before ending the conversation. I know I've got rid of him. That's it now: with or without money, I promise myself I'm leaving this place as soon as possible.

Chapter 23

Exile

19 April 2007

I CAN'T SIT STILL in front of my Spanish set text. It's five o'clock and this is the last lecture I'll attend at V University. Yesterday evening I bought my train ticket to Paris. I'm leaving tomorrow on the 12.47 train and I'll be in the capital two hours later.

Sitting here looking at my work I've got an unbearable urge to cry. I can't believe it will all be over this evening. In two hours' time I won't be a proper student any more, I'll be running away. It doesn't matter how many times I remind myself that, in my current circumstances, I don't have any choice and I really have to leave, I still feel I'm giving up and I see it as a failure. Once again, I haven't seen a year's education through to the end; it feels like my fate's catching up with me, like I'm not designed to sit at a desk listening to someone teaching. Not that my present situation is anything like my last year at school, but I can't help it, I feel it's weak of me to leave.

The ticket was expensive because I don't have a student card, but if that's the price I have to pay to be safe then I'm happy to break open the piggy bank. The hardest thing of all is abandoning uni. I can't get used to the idea. I like the day-to-day student life; I like going to uni every day to learn. In spite of everything I've had to do to be here, I've always felt right when I'm on campus. Still, I'm not giving up my course. I'm determined to finish this year whatever it takes, whether or not I'm actually in attendance for lectures. I've never contemplated giving it all up; I've gone to too many lengths this year to fuck it up at the last minute. All those customers, all that struggling and hard work was basically just so that I could go on studying and not abandon ship.

I've had to find someone sensible and trustworthy to send me their notes by post. One of my girlfriends from uni came to mind straight away. I don't know her very well, we're just on the same course. We automatically seem to sit next to each other for virtually every lesson and we get on quite well although we've never met up off campus. I had to invent some half-cooked excuse to explain why I was leaving, stuff about my family. That seemed the most plausible to me. I didn't like lying to her but I didn't have any choice about that either. For a cash advance towards photocopying and postal expenses, she's agreed to send me her notes.

Our homework doesn't count towards the final result and, with my medical certificate, the tutors can't really complain that I'm missing tutorials. Even though I know I'm not actually giving up, I'm still sad. The whole life I dreamed of back in September has fallen apart. I want to cry because I feel like the victim of some miscarriage of justice . . . and because all my hopes have crumbled. I'm planning to carry on with my course by correspondence, but will I manage it? Am I strong enough and disciplined enough?

I handed in my notice at work yesterday. That made me feel heavy-hearted too, not because I was walking out on a job I liked – that definitely wasn't the issue! – but because, in spite of everything, it had offered me a way out. It meant I could get out of the apartment, bury myself in work and stop thinking about my life. Mostly, I got on well with my colleagues, they often helped me when I didn't know how to do something. My boss didn't really ask why I was leaving. He must see students come and go by the dozen every year – nothing odd about that then.

I don't know what lies in store in Paris. Maybe nothing will be any better, maybe I won't last a fortnight there on my own. I know the problems will start straight away. I'll be running all over the place looking for work, and I'm also going to have to get used to living with someone else again – someone I don't know well, too. Worst of all, there won't be anyone to help me and give me support, or pick me up when I'm down. I'm ready to take all that on because it'll be with a view to having a healthier future, working towards something better. All prostitution ever offered me was the worst.

I've been in touch with my mother's friend who I'm staying with but she can't come to the station to pick me up. She lives in the suburbs and she's told me which Métro line to take to get to her. This is only temporary, of course, she's just helping me out. I need to find a roof over my head quickly: anything will do, a flat-share, a scruffy little room under the eaves somewhere. Even when I'm completely demoralised I can't believe anything can be as hard as what I've been through here in V.

I'm still looking at my text, not listening to the lecture. I should be making the most of my last moments in this magnificent amphitheatre, but I've got so many dark thoughts jostling inside my head. I'm thinking about this evening and my packing, which I'll have to do all on my own. About the work and books I'll have to take with me so that I can carry on studying. They mean so much to me that I wouldn't leave them behind for anything in the world, even if my case weighed a ton. And, anyway, clothes aren't as important, I've managed well enough without new things this year. Since September I've had to learn to prioritise more than ever.

I'm keeping my apartment till the end of the month, because I've paid the rent. It'll be empty but never mind. My father's going to come and pick up the furniture with a friend later. When I let my landlady know I was leaving she obviously wasn't overjoyed but I promised I'd try to find another tenant for her straight away. She's never much liked me and I can't say I blame her. I've often been late with the rent despite all my efforts. I've put ads at uni to say there's a studio available for rent. It shouldn't be hard finding someone in V, even at this stage in the year. Actually, I couldn't give a stuff. I've got plenty of other things to worry about at the moment.

I've only got ten minutes of the lecture left. People are getting restless, wanting to go home. I'd like to cling to my seat and not have to leave. There's no way they'd understand. They couldn't imagine for one second what I've had to do this year to cope with my constant financial problems. The general hubbub is masking the lecturer's voice and, resigned to the fact, he decides to bring the lecture to an end. Once it gets to this time of day, he must know that students' brains become hermetically sealed to all new information and they need to get some fresh air.

People start jumping to their feet the minute they hear him say, 'See you next week.' By force of habit, I sling my worksheets into my bag too. Then I stand up slowly, put on my jacket and walk out of the amphitheatre as if it was just an ordinary day.

Outside, I hug my friend who's going to send me her notes. She wishes me good luck with a hint of sympathy in her eyes. I've lied to her about why I'm leaving but I'm still entitled to her sympathy.

Deep down, I tell myself it's not weak of me to be leaving. Quite the opposite: it's a sensible decision, there are far too many risks in staying in V now. I don't really belong here any more. If I stay I'll never get out. If I leave I do have a chance to reinvent myself. Everything's become impossible here.

I give my friend a wink and head off towards the Métro, just like at the end of any other day.

Chapter 24

Beginnings

24 April 2007

IT'S UNBELIEVABLY HOT in Paris for April. I packed in such a panic I couldn't bring all my summery clothes. I don't really care. It's hot and I've achieved my goal – leaving V.

The struggle has started again straight away just as I predicted. My two aims are, first, to find work, then when I'm settled, an apartment. I'm giving myself two weeks to land a job, any sort of job. After that I'll have to accept that I've failed and go back to V. I can't abuse the hospitality offered by my mother's friend, Sandra.

Just the thought of having to set back to V sends a shiver through me and makes me even more motivated to find something as soon as possible. I haven't stopped for a whole week: armed with my CV, I've been through all the restaurants and small ads to find work ... and fast, so there isn't time for that horrible solution to suggest itself again. So far I've been strong, carried along by the huge sense of hope that Paris is my 'land of exile' where no one knows me as a prostitute, where I can go back to square one and start a new life.

Living with Sandra is going well for now. She welcomed me with open arms, happy to have some company in her apartment. She was once very close to my mother and so was delighted to get to know her daughter. Now in her fifties, you can read all the suffering in her life on her face. She works all day as an accountant for an electrical appliance company and hates her job. She often comes home tired, fed up with her colleagues and the endless numbers she's had to sort out all day. Even so I think she's pretty, especially when she gets home from work and coils her highlighted hair up into a makeshift chignon. She lives a quiet little life, and doesn't want for anything but is far from rich. There's nothing luxurious about her apartment, most of the furniture is second hand, but she's managed to make the place nice with plenty of warm colours.

We often have supper together and she even helps me write covering letters with job applications. One evening she tells me she went through the same hard slog as me in the first few years after leaving university. I wonder whether she ever considered prostitution as a last resort. Weirdly, I would find it sort of comforting if she had, I would feel I wasn't the only one.

I feel happy with her, even though I miss my independent life in my own apartment. She's rearranged her living room so that I can sleep on the sofa bed. Every morning I politely pack it away, not wanting to disrupt her life any more than I have to.

Since I've been here I haven't really been able to concentrate on looking for an apartment. Because I don't have work, I can't provide any sort of guarantees to put my case forward so I'd be bound to be turned down. I'd rather do things in their own time, although I realise that's just what I don't have – time. In spite of everything, Sandra's kindness makes me not want to stay too long. I know from experience that the relationship between two people falls apart more quickly than you think in this sort of situation where one of them is indebted to the other. I feel uncomfortable enough being dependent on someone, I couldn't bear to make her feel uncomfortable about having me here.

I'm back to worrying. I'm alone in Paris, a long way away from friends and family, with no one to lean on for help and support. I need to reach a decision soon: should I go back to V and admit defeat or take action here in Paris? I opt for action. I can't bear the thought of going back to V. I've been through much worse than this in my life, I can keep going now.

So far no one's called me back about work. It's been a week now and I'm beginning to panic. My pockets are empty and I'm not sure I'll make it through this week with what little money I managed to bring with me.

My past is also catching up with me. Joe won't stop hassling me. He leaves me messages every day begging me to go back to V, saying he'll pay my train fare. He says he needs to see me again before he dies. He's offering such exorbitant amounts of money it's becoming unrealistic. I filter all his calls and avoid all his tricks: if my phone rings with a withheld number I just don't answer. I have to admit that, more than once, I've been tempted to give everything up and go sniffing after that money.

I so badly want to draw a line under my past but it's becoming more and more clear to me that I won't be able to without talking about it. I can't get to sleep at night, tossing and turning in bed with horrible images spooling through my head. I often cry, knowing I'm going to have to come to terms with these experiences for the rest of my life. Talk, yes, but who to? I trawl through internet forums devoted to student prostitutes, but never find the answers to my questions. In fact, some girls who use these sites have a go at me for daring to suggest that prostitution is a real scourge among students. I can't believe the things they say, their feelings are on such a different planet to mine that I soon don't even bother logging on, and I give up on these sites as a possible way of freeing myself psychologically.

During my bouts of insomnia I find my only refuge in writing and studying. My evenings and nights, when all is quiet, are devoted to telling my story and describing my emotions. I write for hours on end, not thinking about anything. I'm gradually realising that it's exorcising all the evil eating me up inside. The more I rattle away on my keyboard – on the laptop Joe gave me – the easier it is for me to take a step back from my life. I'm beginning to see a glimmer of hope, to believe I will extricate myself one day. Maybe I really will never be a whore again.

I'm also working harder than ever on my course, even more than when I was actually there in the amphitheatre in V. I don't want to ruin everything, my future seems so uncertain right now. This week I got the first set of notes through the post and they made me so happy. My friend from uni hasn't forgotten about me. I keep my hopes up as best I can: if I manage to find a good job in Paris, I'll put some money aside and enrol at a uni here. I'm sure I can do it. My turbulent life has made me all the more determined. I know what it's like to struggle and I don't want to slip back into that. Sometimes I also cry when I'm confronted with a difficult exercise or a text I just don't understand. I tell myself that my dad's right, I've never done things properly. Maybe not, but I've done my best with what I had, which was almost nothing. People may reprimand me and judge me but I can't turn the clock back. No, I've only ever lived for my future, I only turned to prostitution so that I could carry on studying. They may judge me, yes, but I've never given up.

I'm not going to let myself get depressed now, I've got too much to do and to get on with. Too many things to achieve.

Chapter 25

Dependence

May 2007

THIS LAST MONTH in Paris has been intense. My search for work bore fruit after two weeks, bang on the limit I'd given myself. In the end I managed to get a job as a waitress in a smart restaurant in the middle of Paris. I'm still living with Sandra and the commute to work is exhausting but at least I'm earning money. I make the most of the long Métro journeys to read the work I've put in my bag before setting off in the morning. I force myself to concentrate even though I can hardly keep my eyes open. My hours vary a lot and sometimes I finish late at night after the Métros have stopped running. The first time it happened I took a taxi. I didn't really have any choice. I don't know my colleagues well and couldn't see myself asking if anyone could put me up for the night. When I saw the price clocking up on the counter I promised myself I'd never do it again. It wouldn't make sense to spend all the money I earn on taxis to get home.

I'm confronted with a vicious circle again: I've got a job, yes, but I won't be able to hang on to it for long if I can't sort out these late nights. So I'm trawling through the small ads looking for somewhere to live. As far as prices go, I thought I'd seen how bad it can get in V but Paris is a whole different story. I can't find anything in my tiny price range, not even a miserable little room. Flat-shares can be more affordable but they want lots of guarantees, sometimes even more than for an apartment. I suppose landlords have to put more pressure on sharers to pay on time: the more tenants there are, the higher the risk of not getting their hands on their money.

In the early days Sandra kept saying, 'Just don't worry about it, you can stay here as long as you like, you're no trouble at all!' When she saw that I really needed to live near my work she started helping me as best she could. She asked friends and acquaintances if anyone had a room free. Nothing, not even a rabbit hutch!

Her kindness has gradually changed to ordinary politeness. As my efforts to find an apartment have failed, she's got more and more distant with me, which is only human. We don't eat together any more and she doesn't speak to me much. As predicted, she's beginning to find it a pain having me here. I can tell I'm disrupting her day-to-day life. Her apartment's not very big and the fact that I'm taking up the living room doesn't help much.

One evening I come home from work very late, as usual. I'm exhausted and there's only one thing I want:

to go straight to bed. I find her in the living room with two friends, chatting over a glass of wine having had supper together. When she sees me Sandra pulls a face which says it all: she'd much rather I wasn't there so she could enjoy being with her friends. I feel terrible and try to make myself invisible, slipping off to the bathroom for a shower. When I get back out her friends have left.

'Have your friends gone home?'

'Yes, we couldn't go on chatting here because this is where you sleep.'

I've overstepped the limit of what she can tolerate. Without a word, I open out the sofa bed and get into it. I know that I'll have to leave tomorrow, before Sandra throws me out in exasperation.

At work I ask one of the other girls, who has a big apartment in central Paris, whether she can put me up. We get on well and I know she won't say no. I hate this sort of situation.

'Not for long, just till I find something suitable.'

She agrees with a smile. It's often like that at first, people say yes, glad that they won't be alone any more, but after a while they realise they're better off with their own creature comforts. And in Paris, where apartments are mostly very small, you're always getting under each other's feet. I know this is only a temporary solution and I'll have to find something else quickly. For her sake, but also for mine. I can't be and don't want to be dependent on other people any more.

I pack my bags when I get home that same evening. Sandra hugs me, surprised I've made a decision so soon.

She probably feels sorry for me too, and might feel guilty. But I know that when I'm gone she'll do what she hasn't been free to do for a month: collapse on the sofa and enjoy having the place to herself.

My constant tail chasing often brings back my dark thoughts. What if I gave it all up? What if I accepted Joe's suggestions? I'd get out of this hell. I know deep down that isn't a solution, or only a temporary one. It shines out because of all that money on offer, but when you get closer it looks dirty and dangerous.

I call my friend from uni who sends me notes, to give her my new address. Once again, she doesn't question what I'm up to. Thank goodness, because there's no way I could come up with a new lie for her. She's right in the middle of revision and is beginning to stress about exams coming up.

'Laura, you are coming back to take your exams, aren't you? I could put you up if you like.'

I say of course I am, and thank her for her offer, which I'm going to have to accept because I haven't got anywhere else to go for our exam week in May.

So now I have to negotiate with my boss at the restaurant, and work twelve hours a day for a fortnight to compensate for the week I'll be away. With all the extra hours, I can take five days off. Exactly how long I need to sit my exams.

I let my mother know I'm coming back, but tell her I won't have time to go home and see her, or my father. I can tell she's very disappointed, but at the same time I know that in her heart she's proud of this daughter who never gives up and faces up to her responsibility.

The exam week finishes me off. There's just one thing I want: to lie down on a bed and sleep for hours and hours, and stop worrying about all this. Even so, I don't stop for a minute and work late into the night with my friend. We motivate each other. The human body is adaptable, and the fact that I know the university year will soon be over stops me dropping with exhaustion now. I so badly want to succeed this year, it would be too unfair – after everything I've been through – if I don't. I've done too much studying and too much revising to collapse in a heap at the last minute. I won't let it happen. I've given my all this year, even my own body. No way am I going to fail.

After the exams I say a huge thank you to my friend for taking me in and being so supportive, and I hop on a train for Paris. She didn't ask any questions, obviously feeling my private life was my own business.

I go straight back to work, still at the same hectic pace. I don't even have time to think about how the exams went or my results. I did my best, now all I can do is wait.

A couple of weeks later I'm sitting in front of my computer waiting for the results to come up. I've had today's date buzzing inside my head for a fortnight. I type in my student number; in a few seconds I'll be able to access my results. I'm shaking, I'm so stressed. What if I've failed? Maybe my essays weren't persuasive enough. The fact that I was so tired and fed up might have shown in the things I wrote . . .

All at once the result's there. I've passed, I've got a B+. I'm sitting in front of my computer with tears of happiness rolling down my face. Everything I've been through this year hasn't been in vain after all.

Chapter 26

Hope

5 September 2007

SO I PASSED MY FIRST YEAR exams and I'm still in Paris. I'm nineteen years old and it's the start of a new year. I've carried on working at the restaurant all through the summer, trying to put aside as much money as possible. I'm still living with my colleague and, contrary to expectations, it's going pretty well. I give her everything I can towards the rent which helps her out a bit with her expenses. Our flat-share is nothing like the arrangement I had with Manu. She's struggling too; she understands me.

I talk to my parents on the phone frequently: our relationship has changed a lot. I had to grow up much faster than most people last year, and it shows in the way I behave. I can tell I've got their support. I know from my mother that my father was impressed by my courage and the fact that I passed my exams. They've never understood why I left and I hope they never will. I also know they regret the fact that they still can't help me financially, but their moral support gives me a lift. They're now proving what I've known all along: that they'll always be there, whatever choices I make.

I'm still looking for somewhere to live though. I'm going to enrol for my second year of uni in Paris and I want the right sort of conditions to get on with my work. I don't want to go back to V. Everything's been mapped out in advance for me there, I know that. And I don't want to go on abusing my friend's kindness. The restaurant have offered me an open-ended contract for a part-time job, and I've accepted it. With that guaranteed salary I would imagine things will be easier.

But it's proving harder than I thought. Trailing round looking at studios and garret rooms, I soon realise my case doesn't hold much weight compared to other people's. I don't have any guarantors and, even with a work contract, landlords are happier handing over the keys of an apartment to someone who's got a back-up in case things go wrong. That's what I don't have. Apparently, my parents aren't making enough money. It's no joke.

My future is still uncertain then. I've got a head full of dreams but society keeps bringing me back to reality. I want to carry on with my course, I want to go on learning, but there are always obstacles in my way. Will I manage to find an apartment? Will I be able to combine work and studying? But, most importantly, will I be strong enough to resist slipping back into prostitution?

Money from sex is too quick and there's too much of it for me not to think about it. I know what I want, but I also know it doesn't always fit in with the real world. Big hopes but small means.

Postface

Eva Clouet[1]
Student Prostitution
in the Internet Age

'In France nearly 40,000 students (of both sexes) turn to
prostitution so that they can carry on with their studies.'
This statistic was released by the SUD-Étudiant union in
spring 2006 to counter a movement opposed to the
'equal opportunities' law, and was intended to draw the
French government's attention to the realities of student
life. Of all its arguments, this union has highlighted the
difficult living conditions currently experienced by a
certain proportion of students (the scarcity and costliness
of accommodation, their very restricted budgets, the
difficulties of combining salaried work with university
courses, etc.), and it points out the contradictions in

1 Eva Clouet, 23, is in the second year of a master's degree in sociology –
  'Gender and Social Politics'.

solutions suggested by state organisations to circumvent these problems.

In autumn 2006 the media (particularly the press and television) picked up on this information and brought the issue of students' precarious economic situations into the public eye in a new, vote-catching light. In the context of pre-electoral campaigning, that '40,000' was something of a cat among the pigeons. Curiosity, surprise, indignation, incomprehension, scepticism, fantasy . . . the subject of student prostitution stepped onto the public stage, provoking much debate and mixed reactions.

In our society, whatever form prostitution takes, it remains highly stigmatised and prostitutes[2] are still perceived in the collective imagination as 'marginal' figures because they are 'reduced to selling their bodies'. When it comes to student prostitution, the feeling of unease is only amplified. The image we have of a prostitute – a foreign woman waiting for clients on street corners[3] – seems incompatible with the way we perceive students. And yet, as Laura's testimony proves, student

2 We have used the term 'prostitute' to mean men, women and transsexuals who offer sexual services for payment.

3 In February 2006 138 second-year students of psychology and medicine at Nantes University completed questionnaires about non-student and student prostitution. The results of the study show that, according to this sample, the 'typical profile' of a prostitute in France is 'a young (84.4 per cent of those questioned), foreign (82.6 per cent) woman (97.8 per cent) who solicits on the streets (71.3 per cent)'. This 'profile' mirrors the one portrayed fairly regularly in the media – particularly when referring to prostitution rings – while putting the emphasis on the most visible form of prostitution (where the soliciting takes place in public). In fact, according to the work of (the Nantes branch of) the 'Prostitution Mission' of Médecins du Monde, street prostitution only involves 40 per cent of overall prostitution in France.

prostitution is very much a reality in France. Why is it then that in a major world power whose education system – although criticised with good cause – is often cited as a fine example, some students should have to turn to prostitution?

To date there has been no serious study to put an accurate figure on the scale of the problem – the oft quoted '40,000' is not based on any scientific investigation and is therefore merely an estimate – but Laura's story and my own study of the world of student escorts bring certain elements to light and offer a number of keys to understanding the huge question of student prostitution.

1. STUDENT PROSTITUTION, A COMPLEX REALITY

In the present day there are as many different social categories[4] of prostitute as there are places in which prostitution takes place and ways in which a person can prostitute themselves. With this in mind, the anthropologist and political analyst Janine Mossuz-Lavau explains that it would now be more appropriate to refer to 'prostitutions' in the plural rather than 'prostitution', 'because the circumstances are so diverse'.[5] Each location (studio apartments, bars, nightclubs, the internet, massage parlours, motorway services, woods, camper vans . . .) corresponds to a particular version of prostitution

4 Recognisable groups such as students, young middle-class etc.
5 Janine Mossuz-Lavau and Marie-Elisabeth Handman, *La Prostituion à Paris*, Paris, Editions de la Martinière, 2005, p. 13.

with its own key players, its own codes, specifics, rates, clients, restraints and risks. Of course, students who turn to prostitution are also subject to this diversity. So some students may choose to work the streets[6] while others solicit on campus or in 'small ads', and receive clients in their student halls of residence, and still others prostitute themselves in alcoves in much publicised 'hostess bars' (also known as *bars à bouchon*) or 'massage parlours', and some – like Laura – elect to use the internet to sell their sexual favours. Student prostitution is, therefore, not a homogenous reality since it covers a diversity of forms and practices.

Even so, the democratisation of access to new means of communication – such as Minitel in the 1980s and the internet and mobile phones now – seems to have intensified the development of 'amateur' (as opposed to 'professional') and 'occasional' prostitution, areas in which the student category is fairly visible.

Amongst the many different facets of student prostitution, this postface is intended to shed some light on a particular form of prostitution – the very form practised by Laura – and that is voluntary prostitution, exercised independently (without a pimp) and sporadically by students using the internet.

6 As cited in the testimony of Sélénia (a student who worked as a prostitute for a year on the streets of Toulouse) in E. Philippe, '*Etudiante, je me suis prostituée*', published in the monthly *Esprit Femme*, February 2007, 21, pp. 56–7.

The Internet and Student 'Escort Girls'

In the world of prostitution, the Minitel of the 1980s with is famous *'messageries rose'* and now the internet offer not inconsiderable advantages as much to clients (demand) as to those wanting to prostitute themselves (supply). Apart from the diversity of choice and constant updating, the internet means that – at any time of day or night, in any place and at minimal cost – people can meet discreetly with complete peace of mind because it provides 'comfortable and reassuring anonymity'.[7] Furthermore, the internet naturally makes the work of the police more laborious: 'Prostitutes operating via the internet risk very little because, although they could be pursued for soliciting, they do not constitute a priority for the police.'[8] In the light of this, many former street prostitutes and other 'anonymous' ones – including students – are turning to this area of activity for themselves.

The most visible offers of paid sexual services on the internet are for 'escorts'. Originally, this service simply meant acting as an escort for a client, accompanying someone (usually a man) to parties, restaurants, theatres . . . In this situation, sexual activities are not included in the contract but are still implicitly possible, considered a private act between the escort and his or her client. This

7 Pascal Lardellier, *Le Coeur Net – Célibat et amour sur le Web*, Paris, Belin 2004, p. 65.
8 Extract from production notes by the writer and director Yann Reuzeau for his play *Les Débutantes – Prostituées en quelques clics*, which ran from November 2006 to February 2007 at the Manufacture des Abbesses in Paris.

213

ambiguity explains the fact that escorts are often compared to 'high-class prostitutes', because they fulfil a
specific requirement. 'They are expected to be charming,
attractive and distinguished, but also to have intellectual
qualities suitable for escorting clients who often move in
elevated social circles.'[9] This sort of 'accompaniment'
activity still exists and is mostly handled through agencies, but the term 'escort' is now used by virtually all
prostitutes operating on the internet, whatever 'level of
service' they may be offering. As a result, the word
'escort' covers a variety of meanings: 'Former street
prostitutes driven off their patch, professionals with
diaries full of appointments, foreigners exploited by
prostitution rings[10] or even occasional "call-girls".'[11]

Escorts, whether they are 'professional' or 'amateur'
like Laura, solicit and communicate through advertisements on specialised or more general websites which

9 Christelle Schaff, *Prostitution en France: l'enquête*, Éditions de la Lagune,
  2007, p. 50.
10 Obviously, not all prostitutes on the internet are independent: many work
  for 'agencies', some under constant pressure from pimps, particularly
  where 'tours' (to all intents and purposes slavery rings) have been arranged.
  When a prostitute is 'on tour' she works for a pimp who installs her for a
  set time in a hotel in a large Western city, and she serves a substantial
  number of clients (often more than ten) every day before he moves her on
  to another town. All the recruiting (usually in Eastern bloc countries) and
  soliciting is carried out via the internet. In May 2000 a complementary
  department was set up within the OCRETH (Office Central de Répression
  de la Traite des Être Humains) to tackle criminality associated with
  advances in technology. This body, the OCLCTIC (Office Central de Lutte
  contre la Criminalité liée aux Technologies de l'Information et de la
  Communication), is responsible for overseeing minor offences as well as
  crimes involving immoral earnings of 'pimping'.
11 Matthieu Franchon and Andreas Bitesnich, '*Salariées le jour*, escort girls *la
  nuit*', published in the weekly *Choc*, 28 June 2007, 87, pp. 26–33.

have sections called 'rencontres vénales' (meetings for payment) or 'rencontres pour adultes' (meetings for adults). These advertisements essentially give precise information about the services offered. They might include, for example, the escort's body measurements, age, availability, rates and the area in which he or she works, and occasionally a brief paragraph detailing his or her services as well as 'taboos'.[12]

A fair number of escorts also have their own website or blog. These personalised sites are generally fairly rudimentary in design and interface, and most follow a standard layout. First a window opens and makes it clear that the surfer should be eighteen or over to investigate further. Once inside the site, there is a text – often written by the escort herself – describing her in some detail. Some restrict themselves to physical descriptions while others refer to their interests, marital status and the reason they have turned to prostitution . . . This text also gives the escort an opportunity to reveal her expectations of a paid appointment with a client and of the client's behaviour (how, when and where they can meet, views on sexual practices, type of client . . .). Then a number of different headings are used to pinpoint the exact service offered by the escort. Usually, there is a list of acceptable services and one of those the escort refuses to practise; her rates (by the hour, for an evening, the whole night or more); availability ('work schedule'); and lastly a contact

12 In escorting jargon 'taboos' are sexual practices the escort refuses to perform in the context of sex for money. Conversely, the expression 'no taboos' indicates an escort prepared to accept every kind of practice.

page where the escort gives her email address and/or mobile number. Very often there is a 'photo gallery' to illustrate the blog and show the escort in various different lights. It is true to say that very few 'non-professional escorts' show their faces in these photographs. Generally speaking, those who choose to hide their faces do so essentially to disguise their identity because their friends and family are unaware of their activities as a prostitute and/or escorting is not their only occupation. These women often have another 'official' occupation (as a student, for example) and turn to prostitution occasionally (a few times a month).

For these 'occasional prostitutes' – whether they are secretaries, housewives, solicitors, unemployed, students, etc. – their prostitution remains secondary. 'Occasionals' are therefore mostly independent (working for themselves) and their activities as prostitutes are undertaken as a personal choice – made under difficult circumstances no doubt but none the less a rational choice. Almost inevitably, as Malika Nor[13] points out, occasional independent prostitutes are generally not recognised as such by social services (and that, in fact, is why no organisation – whether institutional or an association – has a clear idea of real statistics for student prostitution). The author adds that this sort of 'voluntary prostitution is usually motivated by money, either because the practice proves extremely well paid and lucrative, or because it only represents a complementary source of income or one needed as a vital minimum'.

13 Malika Nor, *La Prostitution*, Paris, Le Cavalier Bleu, 2001, p. 54.

The choice of prostitution – and the possibility of leading a 'double life' – is unquestionably facilitated by the internet. According to Yann Reuzeau's analysis, 'nowadays, a good many prostitutes start out on the internet. Of them, a lot would never have done it without this "falsely" virtual opportunity [. . .], because what's really new about the internet is that it opens up this profession to absolutely anyone. A basic computer, an internet connection, a couple of photos, fifteen minutes tops and bang, you're an escort!'[14] In fact, by referring back to Laura's testimony, we can see that it is precisely by surfing the internet that students so quickly and easily stumble across a multitude of explicit small ads. Driven by curiosity and a need for money, while still feeling 'protected' behind her computer screen, it is on the internet that Laura finds '[the] solution [. . . she's] been looking for. A bit of comfort, and soon.'

At first sight, it may seem surprising to find students on the prostitution circuit. And yet we know that the student population is far from 'rolling in money', and that many of them have to have jobs alongside their university obligations.[15] Furthermore, a large proportion of work on offer compatible with a student's timetable is not very lucrative, or even underpaid. It is, therefore, hardly surprising that 'for a young person on a fragile

14 This sort of voluntary amateur prostitution is in fact the subject of Reuzeau's latest play *Les Débutantes – Prostituées en quelques clics*. It features Marion, a 19-year-old student of medicine who occasionally prostitutes herself via the internet to pay her way through university.

15 According to the Observatoire de la Vie Étudiante (OVE), in France 47 per cent of students have salaried work alongside their studies and 15 per cent of them work at least six months of the year on at least half time.

financial footing, it is very tempting when you consider the draw of the sums involved in this sort of activity'.[16]

2. WHAT SORT OF STUDENTS PROSTITUTE THEMSELVES VIA THE INTERNET?

It is difficult to establish a 'typical profile' of students who prostitute themselves via the internet. There is however one point that emerges clearly within this population: virtually all the advertisements online are from girls. In fact a close inspection of press articles on the subject in the last twelve months reveals that journalists make no reference at all to male student prostitution. For many people, practising prostitution is 'a woman's thing' and, by extension, student prostitution concerns only female students. Granted, advertisements from male student prostitutes are as good as absent from the Web but that does not in itself mean that male student prostitution does not exist.[17] If we accept this, then rather than thinking of prostitution as 'reserved' for

16 Christelle Schaff, *op. cit.* p. 140.
17 As part of my research I met a young male student who worked as a street prostitute for two years and now uses the internet – deemed '*safer than the street*' – to find clients. He does not have an advertisement or blog, but logs on to gay sites to make new contacts. He feels that the fact that men – and therefore male students – are under-represented as 'providers of paid sexual services' is a question of supply and demand. '*The male demand for "free" heterosexual sex is greater than the supply* – hence the institution of female prostitution to compensate for this discrepancy. *On the other hand, there is a much smaller discrepancy between the supply and demand for "free" male homosexual sex. There are, therefore, fewer male prostitutes than their female counterparts because what they are offering competes with "free options".*'

women, perhaps we should ask ourselves about this difference between the sexes. If then, in prostitution, women are over-represented in terms of supply and men are over-represented in terms of demand, this derives from the fact that prostitution is anchored in a complex unequal system of gender relations. In this system, female sexuality (a social construct) stays under the control of male 'sex drive' (perceived as 'natural' when it too is a social construct). Acknowledging this mechanism of domination and power by men over women is a crucial part of understanding the occurrence of prostitution as a whole and the question of female student prostitution.

Having said that, we do know that the majority of student prostitutes are female. Furthermore, according to various journalistic sources consulted on the subject, female students who turn to prostitution essentially do so because they need the money and do not have enough time to take on sufficiently well paid work while continuing with their studies. In order to explain the choice of prostitution, the media put the emphasis on students' precarious financial situations in the face of a constantly rising cost of living. These are in fact the very reasons that drove Laura to prostitution. Like many students at university, Laura comes from an average background and her living standards depend heavily on those of her family. According to institutional criteria and definitions, though, her family is not 'in need' because both her parents work full time and are paid incomes deemed 'adequate' to provide for the whole family's needs. In reality, however, even with two people on the minimum wage, many of these 'average' families have to learn to 'tighten their belts' to lead a proper life.

All the same, financial problems – linked to the student's social background[18] – cannot be held solely responsible for students choosing prostitution. Indeed not all students 'struggling to make ends meet' turn to prostitution! And not all student escorts need the money literally to survive.[19] Seen in this context, the image of the 'poor little student girl' put forward by the media requires some qualifying.

3. WHAT MAKES STUDENTS TURN TO PROSTITUTION?

According to my research, students turn to prostitution as a response to a variety of discrepancies (some of them deeply affecting) in their lives. The reasons and motives that drive them towards making the choice can, therefore, vary depending on their experiences, and this in itself contributes to the diversity of student prostitutes.

For some, like Laura, prostitution is first and foremost a means to an end – earning money – so that they can carry on with their studies. For others it represents a sort of 'forbidden fantasy' which allows them to break with

18 Financial help from parents and other family members represents 44.6 per cent of student resources [CREDOC figure, 1992] – Olivier Galland and Marco Oberti, Les Étudiants, Paris, La Découverte, 1996, p. 67.

19 During research, I met two female student escorts for whom financial gain was not the principal aim of their prostitution. Both were (comfortably) supported financially by their parents.

traditional family values. For yet others, it is more to do with taking 'revenge' on men for whom they performed sexual favours for free. From these diverse circumstances (which are by no means exhaustive), three patterns of discrepancy emerge: social and financial discrepancies, discrepancies concerning family morality and discrepancies about love and unpaid sexual relations. Clearly these patterns are not rigid, and some students combine two or three of these elements.

(a) Social and Financial Discrepancies – Students Prepared to Do Anything to Succeed

Some students choose to prostitute themselves to finance their studies, pay the rent or just make ends meet. One of the causes that leads to this practice is undeniably a link with the impoverishment of the student population. On this subject, Guillaume Houzel – chairman of the Observatoire de la Vie Étudiante (OVE) – states that 'In the last few years we have seen growing pressure on students' purchasing power. With the rise in house prices, their accommodation costs have gone up ... but their grants have not.'[20] According to the Dauriac report[21] on the precarious financial position of students,

20 Jean-Marc Philibert, 'La prostitution gagne les bancs de la fac', Le Figaro, 30 October 2006, p. 11.
21 Jean-François Dauriac has been a regional student welfare officer for Créteil (1992–2001) and Versailles (2001–4). In 2000, Claude Allègre – then French Minister for Education – instructed Dauriac to establish the current economic circumstances of French students with a view to setting up a 'student social security scheme'. Jean-François Dauriac, summary of notes from his report, Paris 2000.

100,000 students in higher education live on the poverty line set at approximately 650 euros per month per person. The OVE claims that more than 45,000 students now live in extreme poverty and 225,000 struggle to finance their studies.[22] It is important to remember that this impoverishment affects a particular category of student – those whose parents cannot or do not want to support them financially and who, therefore, have to cope entirely (or virtually) on their own to pay for their own needs and continue with their studies.

Like Laura, student escorts from lower- and middle-class backgrounds currently experience a variety of social and financial shortfalls in their day-to-day student life, and these shortfalls compromise – to a greater or lesser extent – their efforts to pursue a higher education. Now, for these students academic success is of paramount importance. Apart from personal gratification, having a higher education opens up the possibility of building on their ambitions – of 'making something of themselves' – and ensuring they have a more 'comfortable' lifestyle than they have experienced at home. But neither these students themselves nor their families have sufficient financial resources fully to back up these ambitions. In this situation, prostitution emerges as an alternative way of 'following [their] dreams'.

22 Jean-Marc Philibert, *op. cit.* – there are currently 2,200,000 students in France.

A number of authors[23] agree that there is not a level playing field in financing student life and that the – mostly financial – benefits enjoyed by those from wealthier backgrounds but absent for those from less fortunate families means there is inequality of access to higher education. The State, conscious of these 'unequal opportunities', has set up a scheme that can give financial help to a proportion of young people (means-tested grants, ability-related grants, allocated housing etc.), therefore offering them a 'fundamental step up the social ladder'.[24] Still, this system is obviously not without its faults (we should remember that Laura is not entitled to a grant) and only partly covers students' needs. Over five years their inevitable expenses – enrolment fees, social security, accommodation, canteen meals etc. – have increased by 23 per cent while university grants and allocated accommodation have increased by only 10 per cent. In these circumstances, a great many students are forced to take on some form of paid occupation alongside their studies.

In 2003 45.5 per cent of French students undertook paid work during the course of the university year

23 Such as Pierre Bourdieu and Jean-Claude Passeron, *Les Héritiers: les étudiants de la culture*, Paris, Éditions de Minuit, 1989; Raymond Boudon, *L'Inégalité des chances – La mobilité sociale dans les sociétés industrielles*, Paris, Armand Colin, 1979; François Dubet, '*Les étudiants*', in F. Dubet *et al.*, *Universités et villes*, Paris, L'Harmattan, 1994; Stéphane Beaud, *80% au bac . . . et après?*, Paris, La Découverte, 2003; M. Euriat and C. Thelot, '*Le recrutement social de l'élite scolaire en France*', *Revue française de sociologie*, XXXVI-3, July–September 1995, pp. 403–38.

24 In 2006 student aid represented 6 billion euros and affected 2.2 million students. Source: Laurent Wauqiez, *Les aides aux étudiants: comment relancer l'ascenseur social?*, Paris, 2006.

(excluding the summer vacation).[25] By studying a case such as Laura's – she works fifteen hours a week for a telesales company as well as her twenty hours a week of university commitments and time spent on coursework – we can measure the extent to which a 'student job' handicaps her ability to study properly. She is permanently tired and this takes a toll on her health. This real-life case mirrors the findings of the OVE which highlight the fact that taking on paid work at the same time as studying increases the 'risks of failing or giving up'[26] at university. These risks derive from the competing needs – mostly in terms of time – of a 'student job' and the requirements of a university course. It is in fact in these terms, according to the OVE, that we need to accept and understand the precariousness of student life. In this sort of situation, prostitution gives students from less fortunate social backgrounds the opportunity to pursue their studies in more favourable financial circumstances – day-to-day needs such as rent and food shopping are covered – while leaving them enough time for their course work, giving them a chance to pass the end-of-year exams.

This strategy may seem logical, but we should still stop to think about the price these girls from average and modest backgrounds are having to pay in order to have access to higher education and to come out with a

25 Claude Grignon (chairman of the OVE's scientific committee), *Les étudiants en difficulté: Pauvreté et précarité* – report submitted to the Minister for Youth, Education and Research, Paris, 2003.
26 *Ibid.*

degree. Clearly, the social ladder and the path to 'success' are far from egalitarian!

(b) Discrepancies in Family Morality – Students Wanting to Escape Their Shackles

For some students prostitution is not directly related to a need for money, but rather a desire to break away from traditional family values and satisfy 'forbidden fantasies'.

Even though sexuality may not now be completely 'free' because – as with all forms of social interaction – it falls within particular kinds of relationships (between the sexes, different social classes, generations, cultures . . .), it is perceived on the surface as less and less codified.[27] On this subject, Michel Bozon points out that one of the major changes in inter-generation relation-ships between the 1960s and the first decade of the twenty-first century is that 'the parents' generation has now given up setting restrictive norms on the young'.[28] The possibility of having 'a proper youth' (as distinct from childhood) has become increasingly widespread and the 'private autonomy' of the young is universally accepted. As such, parents no longer condemn the fact that their children have active sex lives – which are some-times even lived out beneath their own roofs. Obviously, this does not hold true for every contemporary family;

27 Thomas Laqueur, *La Fabrique du sexe – Essai sur le corps et le genre en Occident*, Paris, Gallimard, 1992.
28 Parents do still keep an eye on their children's sexual activity, particularly in connection with the risk of contracting sexually transmitted diseases or of unwanted pregnancy. Michel Bozon, *Sociologie de la sexualité*, Paris, Armand Colin, 2005, p. 54.

some adhere to traditional values – linked to religious morals – and exercise stricter controls on their children's sexuality.

In these more conservative families, young people approach their sexuality under the watchful eye and supervision of their relations (perhaps even their older siblings). The parents set the rules according to which their children – particularly daughters – have access to activities that are a statutory part of growing up.[29] In this sort of environment, the parents often closely monitor who their children are seeing and how and when they see them, chiefly during their teenage years. By the same token, the whole question of sexuality remains taboo and is rarely tackled in family conversations.

For students growing up in families like this, prostitution is seen as a way of emancipating themselves from the family values and norms. By prostituting themselves, these students differentiate themselves from the parental model, thereby affirming their desire for autonomy. Given their circumstances, they want to establish their part in their own lives – their sex lives, at least – and to be involved in building their personal identities.

(c) Discrepancies About Love and Man/Woman Relationships – Disappointed and Disillusioned Students

For some student escorts, prostitution is a way of compensating for an absence of affection or sexual

29 Michel Bozon, *op cit.*, p. 16.

activity. These young women have often been disappointed in previous relationships and 'freely given' sexual unions in which they feel they were not properly valued. They effectively 'gave themselves for free' to men who were unable to meet their expectations of commitment and mutual recognition. They feel they were 'betrayed' and 'abused' in these relationships because they were never given the respect and consideration they deserved.

Even so, these students want to remain sexually active and to improve their sexuality by learning from new experiences and different sexual practices. Seen in this light, their activities as prostitutes make sense. The money exchanged for sexual favours ensures the situation is clear. These student escorts know that a meeting set up in the context of prostitution will not go beyond the terms of the 'contract', and there is no point in hoping that 'something more' might evolve after the paid appointment. They are, therefore, free to experience the rendezvous in all its intensity and focus on their own sexual pleasure without worrying about what might happen afterwards.

4. WHAT TO THINK?

Whatever reasons and motives drive students to prostitute themselves, the practice cannot be viewed as insignificant. Laura's own misadventures clearly illustrate this fact. Still, if it is a personal choice it belongs – like all choices – in a particular context. No one prostitutes themselves by chance. A need for money, a desire to escape or disillusionment about loving relationships are not in themselves enough to explain the fact that some students turn to prostitution.

According to a study on 'the risk of prostitution among young women',[30] there is a 'seed bed' stage during which a number of dysfunctions – connected to an individual's personal and family background – can 'germinate', and this can lead some young women to prostitution. This study shows that there are a variety of 'dysfunctions' and that they can interact and affect each other. It is frequently a question of 'biographical accidents' (acts of physical, moral or sexual violence), problems of identity and of identifying with parental models, a degree of social isolation, a fragile psychological state, social disqualification of the family, distorted images or perceptions of success, or simply the fact that the individual has acquaintances in the world of prostitution.

Choosing prostitution is, therefore, not the result of one single element, but rather a combination of diverse personal and social discrepancies that affect the individual to a greater or lesser extent. Paradoxically, for some prostitution becomes an alternative that gives meaning to their practices and life choices. The moment when a student contemplating prostitution 'actually does it' has

30 This study, conducted by a French organisation, does not refer to the student population but targets young people aged 18 to 25 whose cases are followed by Social Services and who are in precarious economic and social positions. The youth integration scheme of the ANRS (National Association for Social Re-adaptation), *Le risque prostitutionnel chez les jeunes de 18–25 ans* (initial study), Paris, 1995.

its own particular context, it happens at a particular stage in their lives. This activity may help them get out of a 'tricky' situation but it has its own consequences. To date, no study has followed the trajectory of these individuals and established the repercussions – both to the individual and to society – that this practice may have in the long term.

5. ANY SOLUTIONS?

Resorting to prostitution – whatever form it may take – reveals a degree of malaise in society. We have seen that this practice is embedded deep in a system of social relationships typified by male and financial domination. Confronted with this state of affairs, we can but hope attitudes will change to hold current inequalities in check. We know that education is a key in altering attitudes and yet the measures set up by the authorities to bring about any change in behaviour in this area remain inadequate (not to say non-existent).

The subject of sexuality is still broadly speaking a taboo in our society, and has not shaken off age-old beliefs and sexual stereotypes which imprison men and women alike in specific hierarchical sexual roles. Modesty, the possibility of sexual continence, moderation and an absence of desire are still perceived as 'natural' qualities for a woman. Conversely, desire, aggressiveness and proactivity are defined as the preserve of the male.[31]

31 Michel Bozon, *op. cit.*, p. 25.

If more institutions – and individuals – took into account the aspect of social relationships between men and women in their assessments and actions, then it might be possible for sexuality to be seen in a more egalitarian and libertarian light.

For almost ten years now a succession of governments in power have wanted to 'transform' universities, citing as their official reason the fact that they want to improve students' precarious financial situations. Nevertheless, the various suggested reforms (such as the *réforme* LMD, the 'equal opportunities' law and its much-vaunted Contrat Première Embauche, the more recent law giving universities autonomy etc.) in fact only reinforce existing divisions between students from working-class backgrounds and those brought up in more favourable circumstances. If the government's plans were genuinely aiming for a level playing field for all students, a number of concrete measures would be instituted: aid schemes based on social criteria would be re-evaluated (students such as Laura would then be entitled to grants), the number of places in university halls of residences would be significantly increased, 'student jobs' would be fairly paid and better adapted to the needs and abilities of the individual etc.

But, on the question of both sexual and financial equality, those in power still seem just as unwilling to put a toe in the water . . .